PRAISE FOR RICH HABITS

Using a scientific method to identify why some people succeed and others fail... Dr. Randall Bell's bombshell survey for his new book, *Rich Habits Rich Life*... is landmark research detailing the daily habits of professionals, students, stay-at-home moms, retirees, the unemployed and millionaires. He has scientifically identified the link between everyday habits and many measures of success, making it one of the most significant sociological studies ever conducted! In his book, the result of 25 years of research, Bell masterfully links classic behavioral research with his work on high profile cases ... to reveal why some dive, some survive, and others thrive.
Beverly Hills Times

Rich Habits is filled with wisdom, insight, and practical strategy for happy, productive living. Good for all walks of life, wherever you find yourself on the spectrum ... this book has something to offer.
Jon Wilcox - CEO, *California Republic Bank*

Randall Bell shares with us a winning strategy for being successful in our life. He breaks this strategy down into four easy-to-implement tools to quickly jump start your success. I especially enjoyed the "We" technique because it make a challenging principle easy to understand and implement. Great read, great success tools!
Ed Sykes, Author, Success Coach, Motivational Speaker, *The Sykes Group*

Rich Habits Rich Life should be given to every incoming freshman at orientation. It's a bible of brilliant information that's beneficial in and out of college.
Rudy Chavarria Jr, Founder, *College Web Media*

Bell does a nice job of reminding us of important things that will enrich our lives. His organization of the material into the four cornerstones of "Me We Do Be" is innovative. The challenges presented at the end of each section provide concrete examples of things we can do to benefit ourselves and our communities.
Michael Sanders – CEO, *Pacific Realty Advisors*

With chapters titled: "Stand for Something", "The Next Step for Me" and "Pick a Target" this book isn't all motivation, its advice from someone who has studied behavior at places like Chernobyl, the World Trade Center and on the OJ Simpson trial. ...this book does make you think and Dr. Bell gives a logical approach to someone that is trying to get their life back or in some instances take their success to a new level.
Rick Limpert, Sports Tech Writer, *Yahoo Sports, CBS, Atlanta Journal-Constitution*

Rich Habits is filled with powerful lessons applicable to any age or profession. The concept of "Me We Do Be" builds a foundation for a healthy productive lifestyle.
Michael Tachovsky - *Berkshire Hathaway*

Rich Habits Rich Life provides a concise approach to building and establishing a long-term path to a rich life.
Sherrie Wilkolaski, Editor-in-Chief *Luxe Beat Magazine*

Rich Habits Rich Life teaches us that we all have the brain power and energy to become successful in life, but we must first develop positive habits in order to live a life of abundance.
Adam Seyum - *Music Connection Magazine*

Randall shows us how our preparation can intersect with opportunity to create a life of joy, success and positive impact! Jump aboard the success express with the power of *Rich Habits*. You'll be blessed by the journey through a *Rich Life*. I enjoyed every page.
David Rawles, President of CareerSolutions, Radio Show Host, and best-selling author of *Finding a Job God's Way*

You will want to add this book to your *7 Habits of Highly Effective People* (1989), *The Millionaire Next Door* (1996), and *Now, Discover Your Strengths* (2001) reading list.
Rick Soto, Editor & Principal Analyst, *The Journal for Innovation*

Unlike many self-improvement books that may focus on success in a monetary capacity, *Rich Habits Rich Life* presents case studies that support simple changes in habits and rituals, and these changes can be powerful tools applicable in all aspects of life. The studies are backed by proven scientific data that supports a higher elevation in core values, which in turn yields results in elevating one's health, relationships, finances, and happiness. *Rich Habits Rich Life* is a rich read and a great resource to reflect back on from time to time.
Linda Almini, Founder & Publisher, *Lifestyle Resources Magazine*

Got questions about your life? *Rich Habits Rich Life* meets you at the intersection of intellect, spiritual and philosophical. Dr. Randall Bell leeks the vault combination of unlimited solutions you can tailor and tweak. It's a weekend read that changes your vision to claim personal greatness sitting idle. I'm starting Monday morning with enough excitement to *live* dreams with eyes wide open. *Rich Habits Rich Life* spells out how to improve the conditions in your life by the quality of your thoughts. Begin rewriting your life-script, you just got a new *Lease on Life!*
Francene Marie Morris, KISS 95.1 Executive Producer and Radio Host, *The Francene Marie Show*

Your daily habits may count for more than you think when it comes to being successful. Dr. Randall Bell has analyzed the results of a survey and finds there is a correlation between the two issues.
Susan Yackee - National Radio Host

Randall Bell's latest book is indeed a landmark! In today's turbulent times many are on a paper or material chase and as such have been tempted and pick up bad habits on the way. This new book is a must read to breakthrough for all who aspire success in life and family the right way!
Oliver Ho – Principal, *Institute Global Management*

If you open the book and feel like you should just skim the chart boxes to read the "habits" - DON'T. Reading the whole book gives you a glimpse into the author's mind and true intentions. … it's clear that the author has led a purposeful life and he wants to share that gift with others. Dr. Bell holds many pieces to today's world puzzle in his experiences, and since history often repeats, we'd be fortunate to gain from that wisdom before we repeat any of the major tragedies.
The Suburban Jungle

This landmark research detailed the daily habits of professionals, students, stay-at-home moms, retirees, the unemployed and millionaires - and scientifically identified the link between everyday habits and various measures of success. What is so compelling about *Rich Habits* is that it lets us define what success means to us individually, while looking at the foundational elements that apply to us all.
Sandra Pesmen, *Palm Beach Post and Fresno Bee*

Rich Habits Rich Life gathers research covering the daily habits of a cross-section of successful people, from educators and professionals to full-time mothers, retirees… even the unemployed and the millionaire. While some of these groups have been studied in narrower scope, the unique focus of *Rich Habits Rich Life* is on the behaviors that lead to disaster or prosperity. It creates a powerful study that synthesizes some 25 years of the author's behavioral research. The result is an eye-opener. It is recommended for any inquiring reader who would assess self and surroundings to identify the rituals leading to success.
Diane Donovan, Editor - *Donovan's Literary Services*

While we each have our own definition of success, Dr. Bell's extensive research shows we do share certain foundational elements. His book creates a fresh perspective for success by connecting the dots between the four cornerstones of "Me We Do Be."
Mama Fashionista

Randall Bell has travelled the world and seen many things, good and bad. He has a PhD in Human Organizational Systems and an MBA from UCLA, not to mention 25 years' worth of experience consulting on tragedies around the world … He is also an avid volunteer with youth groups and homeless people, not to mention a married father of four. All of these experiences add up to a life that could leave a man jaded about people and the world. That is not the case with Bell though. I might have to keep this book handy to keep my inspiration up when spirits flag.
Katherine Krige - *A New Day Blog*

Dr. Bell's four-part "Me We Do Be" model put this reviewer in mind of Stephen Covey's habits of highly effective people approach with its four time management quadrants. However, with (this reviewer's) own PhD in Russian language and literature she appreciated Bell's more academic examples from Chernobyl, the 9/11 attacks on the World Trade Center, and other major world events. He favors the blunt all American wisdom of Benjamin Franklin and keeps his historical examples clear and relevant. Any reader at any level should find value in Bell's rich discussion.
Dr. Laura Wilhelm - LauraWil Intercultural

Rich Habits Rich Life is required reading for every college student majoring in business, for every graduate student in an MBA program, for everyone in and running a business, and for all who want to be intelligent and balanced thinkers. Dr. Randall Bell addresses the facts, the practices, and the total person in business so he or she will be complete in any decision-making process. This book ends naiveté, which no intelligent adult can afford to be when desiring success on all levels.
Lindsey Novack - Nationally Syndicated Workplace Columnist

As a navy seal, a complete set of skills are required for a successful mission. What I like about *Rich Habits* is that it lays out the framework for a complete game plan. This is a great book for anyone who wants an advantage in life or business!
Peter Skeehan, *Former Navy Seal*

Rich Habits sets forth a complete, intelligent framework. It cuts through the fluff of most self-development books and delivers proven strategies for both individual and organizational growth.
Michael L. Lowe, PhD - Professor, *Georgia Tech University*

While television shows are a lot of fun, they are also a lot of work. Filming a successful television show takes both physical and emotional balance. I really enjoyed *Rich Habits* because it skips the hype and reveals the habits and routines that we all need to be successful.
Geri Jewell – Actress, Star in NBC's *Facts of Life*

Rich Habits
Rich Life

Rich Habits
Rich Life

The Four Cornerstones of
All Great Pursuits

Randall Bell, PhD

Leadership
Institute
Press

Leadership Institute Press
Laguna Beach, California

RichHabits.com

ISBN 978-1-933969-23-7

Library of Congress Control Number 2015951705

Printed in the United States of America

10 9 8 7 6 5 4 3 2 1

Leadership Institute Press titles are available at significant quantity discounts when purchased in bulk. Custom printing is also available.

For details contact bulksales@leadershipinstitute.com

A portion of the proceeds of this book are donated to the Friendship Shelter in Laguna Beach, California. This homeless shelter has a remarkable success rate in helping homeless men and women rebuild their lives, get jobs and move forward with happy, productive lives.

DEDICATION

The major problem today is that many believe in one of the two great lies. The first great lie is that we are perfect and flawless; the second is that we have no hope. While polar extremes, either lie has the same result. Both lies destroy growth.

The solution is to honestly assess the one thing we can actually control: ourselves. Cultivating rich habits, rituals, and routines is the most direct way to a rich life.

This book is dedicated to those who reject the two great lies and have the courage to move forward and continually grow.

Table of Contents

Introduction

What is a winning strategy? Why do some people, families, and organizations take a dive, some merely survive, while others thrive? What leads up to a disaster or collapse? Why do some squander success, while others continue to elevate? How do we build a solid foundation that assures solid, authentic growth?

Rich Habits Rich Life is the result of research that has spanned twenty-five years at the intersection of sociology and economics. Specifically, I have explored what behaviors lead to disaster, recovery, or prosperity.

As an economist, I measure the financial effects caused by disasters and other detrimental conditions. In other words, when disaster strikes, I am often called in to compute the business and real estate damages. Appraisers measure value, but I measure the loss of value. Moreover, also being a sociologist, I keep my eye on the people behind the statistics as I develop the strategies to move forward. It is a narrow consulting niche involving research, valuation, negotiation, and strategy, and it has provided unique access to interesting people and places around the globe.

The journey began in the 1980s when I was a graduate student at UCLA studying leadership and business models. In the 1990s, I directed a national practice at the world's largest consulting firm. My research expanded as I walked the reactors at Chernobyl and cut through the jungles around the Bikini Atoll radioactive nuclear test sites. I have worked on cases ranging from the O. J. Simpson and JonBenét Ramsey crime scenes to the bizarre Heaven's Gate Cult mass-suicide mansion.

In the 2000s, there was more. I was stunned as I stood on a curb in New York and watched smoke billowing from the World Trade Center and picked up debris on a rural field in Pennsylvania where Flight 93 had crashed on 9-11. I walked the beaches stained by the BP Oil Spill and inspected thousands of homes torn apart by Hurricane Katrina.

As a socio-economist I have worked on these and hundreds of other cases around the world. More importantly, I have studied their ultimate resolution. While some reporters drop in and rush off to the next story, I have stayed to talk to the people long after the news vans drive away. Furthermore, I have been an advisor in countless boardrooms where we discussed cases involving billions of dollars.

A crisis exposes a person's or organization's true character, and this yields some invaluable insights. In all, I had accumulated a mountain of information and I wanted to organize it within a practical framework. My objective was to find a model that children could understand and that a CEO would take seriously. I considered using the ancient Greek paradigm of "ethos, pathos, and logos" and a more modern framework of "mental, social, spiritual, and physical." Of course, there was the standard, "mind, body, and soul" as well as many other models.

All of these struck me as good, but none of them struck me as complete. It was as if they were playing some of the keys of the piano, but not the whole keyboard. I simply wanted a clear, complete framework.

My quest for the ideal model ultimately came to me on the Marianas Islands as I sat in deep thought for three consecutive days. The answer was simple: Just as all great structures have four cornerstones, there are four cornerstones of all great pursuits. These can be summed up as *Me We Do Be*.

Me refers to habits that build quality thinking and wisdom, *We* habits build relationships, *Do* habits build productivity, and *Be* habits build the future.

In the pages that follow, I will use this *Me We Do Be* framework as we explore some of the most fascinating places on Earth, learn from the experiences of some extraordinary people, and look at classic behavioral research. This is all set out within the four *Me We Do Be* sections, twenty-one short chapters, and about one hundred individual lessons. The objective of each lesson is to encourage discussion on essential life skills.

On top of that, more than five thousand people from all fifty states, Australia, and the United Kingdom participated in our Rich Habits survey.[1] Here, my research staff and I surveyed professionals, students, stay-at-home moms, retirees, the unemployed, and multi-millionaires. We studied dozens of rituals ranging from writing thank-you notes to eating together as a family. We then statistically correlated various habits with different measures of success such as education, wealth, quality relationships, and an overall sense of happiness.

Obviously, some people define success as making money. I joke that money doesn't make anyone happy, but it's a great way to be miserable! However, some might define success as a happy family life, finding true love, or winning a competition. Some see success as contributing to a worthy cause, completing a degree, or mastering a musical instrument. Others view success as healing from an emotional wound, beating cancer, or connecting with the divine. Some see success as being a leader or building a huge name for themselves, while others just want the satisfaction of quietly doing great work. Many define success as a combination of things.

I respect the perception that there is no one-size-fits-all for success. Here, we define what success means to us individually, but in so doing, we will look at the foundational elements that apply to us all.

The research and science is clear: however you define "success," daily habits, rituals, and routines is the key to either tragedy or triumph. Just as one bad habit rippling out until a life is destroyed, it is also true that one new good habit can ripple out and create something magnificent.

---

[1] The "Rich Habits" survey is one of the largest sociological studies of its kind ever conducted. In all, more than five thousand people from all fifty states participated in sharing their daily habits, routines, and rituals, along with information on their level of education, income, net worth, health, and overall sense of happiness. The study included both multiple choice and open-ended questions where the answers were analyzed using statistical and word-frequency software. All results were evaluated for statistical correlation, ranked, graphed, and placed into the "Me We Do Be" framework. The survey findings were statistically valid with an overall error rate of between 2.5 percent and 3 percent. Some results validate common views, some notions are dispelled while others provide fresh insights into human and organizational behavior.

Today's habits, rituals, and routines are tomorrow's destiny, and minor adjustments bring major rewards. Indeed, the four cornerstones of *Me We Do Be* lay the foundation of every great pursuit. They bring results that are positive, profound, and permanent.

We have absolutely no control over most things, like the weather or the global economy. The only thing we really control is ourselves and the habits we choose. We dictate when we get up, what we eat, what we say and how we think. Focusing on a proven set of rich habits is simply the most direct way to building a rich life.

Chapter 1

The Four Cornerstones

Me We Do Be

The Four Cornerstones

T he world's majestic structures stand as legacies to great empires and civilizations. The medieval castles of Europe, Roman cities, and the Great Wall of China still awe and inspire. The ancient city of Machu Pichu and the Egyptian pyramids are simply baffling. Even the obscure British scientific outposts in Antarctica are impressive as they withstand the harshest winters on planet Earth.

While the great structures include pyramids, cathedrals, towers, and opera houses, they all have one thing in common: The integrity of all these structures comes down to one element—all of the world's great structures sit on a solid foundation.

Not every structure has met this requirement, and cutting corners is disastrous. Indeed, the quality of a building's foundation means the difference between a trophy or a tear down.

Nobody really knows the origins of the term "fair and square," but I believe that it came from the construction of the cornerstones of history's great buildings. "Fair" refers to rock—that it is free of cracks. "Square" means that the stone is perfectly cut to be level and that the corners are at right angles.

Cornerstones were chiseled with one swing of the hammer at a time, just as our life's foundation is constructed with one habit at a time. It is hard work to construct a cornerstone, which then sits underground and goes largely unnoticed. But laying a solid foundation ensures that whatever is built on it will last. It is not easy, but it is worth it. In fact, it is essential.

The four cornerstones are essential foundational principles, summed up in four simple words, *Me We Do Be*. The *Me* habits improve the quality of our thinking and mental illumination. The *We* habits build our relationships. The *Do* habits elevate our health, finances, and living space. The *Be* habits include setting goals, managing our time, and building our legacy.

A five-year-old can understand *Me We Do Be* principles, but I have worked on several multimillion-dollar cases where we followed this same framework. It works because it is practical, complete, and balanced.

The objective of the four cornerstone framework is not to define success. The purpose runs deeper. The four cornerstones are for those who have vitality and want to continually elevate. The ultimate goal is not to become a "success" in terms of accumulating power, prestige, or more "stuff"; but rather, as Albert Einstein says, to become a "person of value."

British psychologist Oliver James describes a society that is obsessed with commercialism and appearances, which comes with a set of related issues such as debt, anxiety, and general life overload.[2] There have always been millions of self-consumed drones who follow the crowd and go through life day-to-day. Some people are content with the status quo. Many simply follow the commercially driven, sugar-coated counterfeits for success.

Others have reacted by downshifting and have made an effort to balance their lives with less income and social climbing, but more focus on family, close friends and those things that bring a general sense of well-being.[3]

Personally, I don't buy into the mass media's definitions of success. The "person of value" has a solid foundation of core principles and virtues, has abundant social connections, takes care of his or her health, space, and money, and ultimately contributes to something bigger than himself or herself.

The four cornerstones renew the focus on those universal laws upon which all achievements are built. As we look at each cornerstone and its corresponding disciplines, we ensure that we are on solid footing.

People who lose their footing cause many of the crises I study. While I have spent decades working on the world's great disasters, that is not my legacy. My passion is to explore the lessons and gain some insights that will help the recovery process.

The four cornerstones set forth the foundation of all great pursuits whether it is art, science, love, leadership, education, sports, religion, politics, parenting, or anything else. These same cornerstones are consistently observed in the personal disciplines of a diversity of high achievers, including Lincoln, Einstein, ad Vinci, Shakespeare, Gandhi, and Washington.

Likewise, these distinct attributes can be observed in the lives of historic religious and philosophical figures including Moses and Jesus, as well as Buddha, Mohamed, Socrates, Plato, and Aristotle. If you look carefully, the four cornerstones are at the foundation of all great lives.

The Anatomy of a Habit

Just as a great mountain is the sum of grains of dust and the vast oceans are the total of small drops of water, so are our lives the sum of our habits and routines. Our tiny actions, good or bad, add up and make us what we are.

Fundamentally, our brain develops habits to save energy. For example, when we first learn to ride a bike, it consumes every bit of our concentration. But once it becomes a habit, it becomes virtually automatic, thus freeing up our minds to watch our surroundings, chat, navigate, and enjoy the ride.[4]

The brain treats all habits the same, and does not distinguish between a "good" habit and a "bad" habit, so we must deliberately choose them. Just like brushing our teeth, a habit is not something we do once or twice and then expect results. Once selected, they must be implemented until they become automatic.[5]

Those habits and virtues we choose have profound consequences. A college friend has always been in the habit of saving and investing money; he just bought his third house and this one sits right on the ocean.

A childhood friend got into the habit of stealing and sits in prison. My parents took care of their health and traveled the world into their nineties. All of these results can be traced back to the culmination of daily rituals.

There has been enormous scientific research on habits, but it essentially comes down to three components, which are:

1. a trigger event or cue,
2. a ritual or routine, and ultimately
3. a buzz or reward.[6]

To understand habits, we must understand this cycle of triggers, rituals, and buzzes. For example, hunger will trigger the routine of eating and the buzz is the satisfaction of being full. A starting trigger and the ending buzz are inevitable; the only thing we can change is the ritual or routine in the middle of the two, such as choosing to eat something healthy or eating junk food.[7] The cues of hunger, boredom, and base desires are inevitable. The question is if we get our buzzes from healthy or unhealthy routines.[8]

As habits become more and more ingrained, they become cravings.[9] In other words, if we choose the habit of eating healthy food, we will eventually crave healthy food. But if we choose the habit of eating junk food, we will develop a craving to eat more and more junk.

A cornerstone habit is a new, single habit that will grow to crowd out the bad.[10] The power of a simple, new cornerstone habit is that it has a ripple effect. Once we master a new cornerstone habit, it inevitably evolves

Dive–Survive–Thrive

When setbacks hit—and they always do—there are only three options. The first is to take a "dive" and let the issue create a permanent setback. The second is to work back to the pre-disaster level and "survive," which is admirable.

The third option is also the most interesting. This is where the setback wakes up unrealized potential and one actually elevates higher than one was before. This is called, "post-traumatic thriving," and is the highest level of human peak performance.

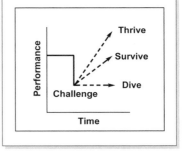

into more and more similar habits.

For example, if someone simply modifies a single habit of eating oatmeal instead of donuts for breakfast, or takes a walk in the morning, those tiny actions will likely ripple out. This person is more likely to make healthier choices throughout the day.[11]

Often we don't need to overhaul everything in our lives or businesses, we just need to carefully select one new habit and let the positive effects naturally spread out from there.

Core IQ

An IQ test, or "intelligence quotient," is a standardized test that measures human intelligence. An average IQ is 100, and about two-thirds of the population scores between 85 and 115. Only about 5 percent score more than 125.

As important as the IQ is, in a context of balance and wholeness there is something far more important. "Core IQ" is the term I have given to the cumulative aptitude that includes intelligence along with philosophical, spiritual, sociological, physical, financial, developmental, and other aptitudes. Understanding this complete perspective can set a tidal wave in motion.

On weekends, I volunteer at our community's homeless shelter where I teach a class on life skills. Soon after starting, I realized that this situation was more than real—it was outright raw. The people who walk in that door have been through every assortment of tragedy and horror.

I have taken a novel approach—I teach the homeless the same executive and leadership skills I teach billionaires. I do this because these are fundamental principles that apply to everyone.

Some homeless people have simply given up, but my class is full of those who want to turn their lives around. I see the determination in their eyes to reboot and fly straight. They don't want to go back on the street or worse—they don't want to end up dead or in jail. At this point, they are not interested in a theory. They need a solid, practical game plan.

To start, I give each new person a challenge coin. Challenge coins are an age-old military practice to carry a coin at all times and to present it when challenged by an officer or fellow soldier. The coin represents a commitment to core values. If you showed your coin, you were respected and saluted. If you didn't, you did pushups.

It may sound trivial to try and help people by giving them a coin and then challenging them to hold onto it, but the principle runs deeper. The people the class have hit rock bottom. Many of them have come from stable backgrounds with family and friends, but their situation has left them largely alone.

Accepting the challenge to simply put the coin in their pocket or purse gives me the hook I need. If there is going to be a turnaround, it can only happen with a new set of habits, rituals, and routines. Yes, some of them cling to their old habits, and it hurts when they go back out to the streets or worse. But most of the time, with a great community effort, we have success.[12]

I remember Danny well.[13] He rolled his eyes in arrogance the first time we met and I handed him a challenge coin. He was angry and ashamed that he had gone from his childhood home in a posh neighborhood to a homeless shelter. He had once been neighbors with Warren Buffet, one of the richest men in the world. Later on, he had some unexpected health issues and had made some mistakes. He thought that he did not belong in a shelter, yet here he was.

Danny came back the next week. I asked him if he had his challenge coin and he sat up straight and announced that he did. I told him that I was proud of him; under the arrogance I could see him hold back a smile. He had not heard anyone say that in a long time.

I tell my homeless friends about my full-glass theory. We all have a story but we have limited time. I joke that they can wallow in that misery with the clinical psychologist who comes in on Wednesdays. I go on to explain that life is like a glass. In life, we have a limited capacity and can only hold so much. If our glass is full of toxic junk, we can treat it, ignore it, or play around in it. Or, we can pour in fresh water until the junk dilutes and is gone.

We take a healthy approach and flood our lives with new, good habits. We discuss the anatomy of a habit, the four types of habits, and examples of rich habits and poor habits. We talk about how bad habits cannot be eliminated; they are replaced with good ones.

From a long menu of good habits, we discuss picking just one. Some of my students get excited and tell me that they want five or ten new habits, but I insist on just one. I don't want what I call the "January 4th Effect," which is about the day when most New Year's resolutions are abandoned. I am looking for easy wins.[15] We want only commitments that we will really keep.

After several weeks, Danny got around to telling me that he was going to develop a new habit and do fifty push-ups a day.

"Danny," I said, "no, your new habit is one pushup a day. You can then do ten or twenty or fifty more if you want, but your only commitment is to do one." So, Danny agreed to do one pushup a day.

Whatever is measured improves.[16] In class, we measure our performance so that we don't fool ourselves. Salespeople sell more when they keep track of their sales calls, students do better when they keep track of their grades, and people lose more weight when they keep a log of everything they eat. The next week, Danny came back to say that he had only done one pushup a day. He looked a little dejected, but I exclaimed, "Great! You kept your commitment and you met your goal!"

The next week, Danny did an average of six pushups a day. I told Danny that it was terrific—he was doing 600 percent more than his commitment. Now Danny had an impossible time trying to not smile.

After a month, Danny was actually doing fifty pushups a day, meditating twenty minutes a day, and writing in his journal. We never even discussed a formal commitment to these other habits, but the one habit had enough kick to ripple out into more and more rich habits.

The only commitment I ever asked from Danny was to carry a coin in his pocket and do one push-up a day. From there I simply facilitated a group discussion about healthy habits. As a result of the efforts from a host of staff and volunteers, soon Danny was deliberately choosing to think positive thoughts, take better care of his health, say "hello" and be friendlier to people, stay out of bars and other slippery places, and a host of other rich habits. He carried himself better, read more books, and earnestly began looking for work.

After steadily rebuilding a new set of habits, Danny got a job and moved into an apartment. He literally went from sleeping in his car, to a homeless shelter, to a happy and productive life. Danny has a new outlook about how he thinks and builds relationships. Danny has gone from being poor to rich.

Danny's success is attributable to his efforts to elevate his entire Core IQ, get past his arrogance, study and think sharper, connect better with others, do his chores and jobs more effectively, and set goals to reach the next level.

Indeed, this elevation of Core IQ is the same formula for anyone who wants to go from a bad place to good or from a good place to a great place

The *Me We Do Be* of Students

The four cornerstones lay the foundation for education. *Me* is the position as a student where they can obtain an education that will benefit them for the rest of their lives. Here, students develop their study habits, intellect, and drive. They can think, explore, ask questions, form their own philosophies, and gain wisdom.

We is connection with people. Here, students connect with their fellow students and their teachers. Students can gain an appreciation for the advanced knowledge that their teachers, mentors, and professors have. They may connect with other students and form study groups where they can synergize and learn even more. Smart students know that the friendships and relationships formed at school can last a lifetime.

Do is productivity. As a team of students, faculty, and study groups, everyone has to be productive. While teachers should produce accessible and intelligent instructions, students should absorb that information and produce on their homework assignments, class presentations, and tests.

Be is progress. On this point, students contribute to the group, help other students, and build the school's legacy. When they finish school, they can be a part of an active alumni group.

Yes, there are students who do not take school seriously, have a hard time connecting with others, don't get their homework done, or blow the joint the second they graduate. Sadly, this mind-set may follow them into the *Me We*

Do Be habits of their careers and parenthood. But smarter students build on those four cornerstone perspectives.

The *Me We Do Be* of Parents

The four cornerstones lay the foundation for moms and dads. *Me* is the position of being a father or mother and gives parents the opportunity to raise their children. Home can be the ideal setting to build wisdom and develop intellectually, philosophically, and spiritually.

We is connection. Here, parents take a genuine interest in their children's unique attributes and gifts. They know their hopes and dreams and want their happiness. Here, parents can really love their children. When parents connect, their children know it and they love their parents.

Do is productivity. Families work together to get things done, and everyone has chores to do. A family can step up for each other. Just last night, my son told me about a science project he had to make a circular span bridge. I did not even know what that was, but we studied bridges and spent the entire evening building one out of Popsicle sticks. It was a great feeling when we got the job done.

Be is progress. On this cornerstone, parents work with their children to build the family legacy. Parents can provide the foundation for their children to one day become parents themselves.

Just as the four cornerstones of *Me We Do Be* apply to students and parents, they apply in business, leadership, and in any other context. In my work with disaster recovery projects, the first step is always to assess the situation. This same principle of assessment works in any situation where we want to elevate and build. The Four Cornerstones of *Me We Do Be* are a powerful tool because they assure a balanced assessment in our thinking, relationships, productivity, and our overall plan to go forward.

SECTION 1

THE *ME* CORNERSTONE

We rise to the level of our illumination

Chapter 2
The *Me* Habits

It's All in Your Head

The construction of every great historic palace, cathedral, and castle started with the chief cornerstone.

The chief cornerstone was not only a critical foundational element, but it marked the precise point from which all other parts of a structure were measured. A survey marker, or benchmark, would be driven into this stone. This is the point of beginning. No matter how simple, large, or elaborate the structure, it all came down to the integrity of the chief cornerstone.

Before there is any decision, there is a thought. Before anything is spoken, there is a thought. Before there is any action, there is a thought. Before there is a relationship, there is a thought. Before there is any progress, there is a thought.

> ### The *Me* Cornerstone
>
> The first cornerstone, *Me*, is the quality of our individual thinking. It is the sum of our intellectual, philosophical, and spiritual illumination.
>
> To build on this cornerstone, disconnect from all distractions. Take time for personal study and reflection on those topics that are most important to you.

And so it is with our lives, careers, or businesses. The key starting point is *Me* and those habits that form our individual way of thinking. If we let garbage thoughts in, the outcome will be garbage. If we invite positive thoughts, we will grow.

Physiologically, when we think a negative thought, our brain literally secretes chemicals into our bloodstream that circulate through our system and make us feel bad. When we feel bad, we think more bad thoughts and the cycle continues. On the other hand, when we choose to stop thinking of something that is negative, and instead think of something good, our brain then secretes chemicals into our bloodstream that make us feel good. These simple choices in our thinking determine our ultimate success or failure. Our thinking, and the level of illumination within our thinking, sets us squarely in the direction we will go.

The *Me* habits are all the things we do to develop our mind-set. This concept of combined thoughts, beliefs, and feelings might be captured in the Latin phrase *fiat lux,* which means *let there be light,* or translated another way, *let light be made.* This phrase goes to the core of intellectual, philosophical, and spiritual illumination.

Fiat lux, and derivations on this theme, is the motto for some of the world's greatest academic institutions including UCLA, Yale, and Berkeley. These were also the first recorded words of God as recorded by all Judeo-Christian faiths. Only when we set aside some time for solitude, clear thinking, and learning can we go forward to achieve something significant. The principle of *fiat lux* might be summed up as those routines that generate knowledge and wisdom.

We love what we serve. Some people do not believe much and thus dedicate their lives to the little or nothing they serve. In the play *Joan of Lorraine,* written about Joan of Arc, these were her words before her death:

> *I know this too now: Every man gives his life for what he believes. Every woman gives her life for what she believes. Sometimes people believe in little or nothing, nevertheless they give up their lives to that little or nothing. One life is all we have, and we live it as we believe in living it, and then it's gone. But to surrender what you are, and live without belief—that's more terrible than dying—more terrible than dying young.*

The *Me* habits tune up and build our philosophical, spiritual, and intellectual core. While some learning happens suddenly, like walking out of a cave into the noonday sun, more often light comes slowly, like morning's dawn. Whether illumination comes quickly or slowly, the starting place for any venture is to turn on the lights and closely examine, question, and investigate one's purpose. To skip such an integral step would be like setting sail without a rudder.

Chernobyl

Me habits generate intelligent and logical thinking. The lack of clear thinking and judgment is at the heart of most of the disasters I study.

The nuclear industry is extraordinarily regulated and controlled.[20] On one hand, nuclear power is by far the most efficient fuel there is. Just one pound of enriched uranium, about the size of a baseball, in theory could power a car eight hundred times around the world.[21] On the other hand, radioactive materials are highly toxic. Mere inhalation of radioactive fumes can kill in less than ten minutes. The regulations, when applied, result in a remarkably safe and powerful energy source. However, rules are of no use to people who are in the habit of breaking rules.

> ### Rich Habit #1
> ### Fly Straight
>
> Of the *Me* habits that people are most proud of, honesty is ranked number one.
>
> | Category | Index |
> | --- | --- |
> | 1. Honesty | 125 |
> | 2. Reading | 87 |
> | 3. Attending church | 28 |

The former Soviet Union had a widespread culture of corruption that, in all contexts, guarantees ultimate failure.[22] In this case, the tragedy occurred at Chernobyl, a small village a couple of hours' drive from the capital city of Kiev in the Ukraine. The village sits across the river from the once large city of Pripyat. The area around Chernobyl is a green and lush countryside with vast fields for growing crops. In many ways the area is a step back in time with beautiful, lush trees, bushes, and meadows. To this day, there are people throughout the region who use horse-drawn wagons to take their produce to market. It was an odd setting for a catastrophic disaster.

Sitting on the Chernobyl side of the Pripyat River was a massive complex of multiple six-story structures that housed four nuclear reactors. Like all such facilities, there was a massive control room that monitored and controlled the entire complex.

On April 26, 1986, a group of scientists gathered in the control room at the Chernobyl Nuclear Power Plant to conduct an unprecedented experiment. They had no authorization and there was no basis for the test that they had concocted. Essentially, they were curious to see if the plant's spinning turbines had enough energy to power an emergency shutdown. Apparently, it never occurred to them to consider the consequences if their test failed.

These scientists broke every nuclear protocol and turned off all seven safety systems. They cut the power to the turbine and then they tried to shut down the reactor.

The nuclear core overheated and, in their frantic response, the reactor exploded with a full-scale nuclear meltdown. If only one of the seven safety measures had been in place, the accident would never have occurred. The initial blast killed dozens of workers, but far more damage was caused when the nuclear fuel caught on fire.

Visually, a nuclear meltdown looks like a small fire; however, inhaling the toxic smoke shuts down the body's central nervous system. As emergency workers responded, many teachers took their students outside to observe the brave firefighters, not knowing that they were actually contributing to the death or injury of their students.

Today, Chernobyl is a ghost town under a blanket of radioactive dust. The seventeen-mile radius "exclusion zone" consists of deserted villages, bulldozed towns and the abandoned city of Pripyat. When I inspected Chernobyl, the government representative and I were the only people in the entire city.

My first impression upon arriving at Chernobyl was that it is an enormous complex of massive buildings. We drove by the two reactors that had been under construction at the time of the disaster. A deserted crane still sat there. We continued past the three operating nuclear generators and then to Reactor 4, the site of the disaster itself. It was strange standing there, alone, next to a six-story gray structure enclosing the greatest nuclear disaster in history.

The accident occurred about a week before May Day, a major holiday in Eastern Europe. Deserted rides, such as Ferris wheels and bumper cars, still stood eerily silent. Radioactive dust was everywhere; no matter where we went, the Geiger counter stuttered continuous fast clicks. Our radioactive exposure still climbed three or four times past the safe limit.

I was given full access to the entire city, so we hiked into overgrown areas to enter a deserted elementary school. Gray, radioactive fallout covered everything—from the colorful cartoon murals, to the pianos, desks, toys, and dolls in their cribs. In one building, I came across a poster that instructed the children on what to do when the Americans bombed Russia. Ironically, it was covered with radioactive dust from their own backyard.

The children's names were still posted on a bulletin board for that day's assignments. I stepped over a pair of white shoes that looked just like a pair my own daughter had back home. In this setting, it didn't take a lot of imagination to envision the children affected by the tragedy. Based on false assurances from their leaders that all was safe, the children inhaled highly radioactive dust, smoke, and fumes. Many died, while others had to have their thyroids removed, resulting in a long scar on their necks called a "nuclear necklace."

This was more than a nuclear disaster. Chernobyl was a failure of basic core values. An unprincipled mind-set is the key to tragedy. In the long run, neglecting basic values invites problems.

Chernobyl started off with some guys at work who had gotten into the habit of thinking that the rules and regulations did not apply to them.[23] They also believed that they were immune to failure. They were just a part of a widespread culture of corruption that spread from top to bottom throughout the country. When word of the tragedy got to the nation's leaders, they too had these same habits. They lied to the world saying that nothing was wrong and that a roof had simply caught on fire.

The Western world was simply not buying the Soviets' story. The international community started detecting large dosages of radiation across Western Europe and outrage grew. Once I attended a conference where Mikhail Gorbachev stated that Chernobyl caused $16 billion in damage. My calculations show that they were not finished counting.

Crisis often brings collapse and a new set of habits.[24] With the world's fury focused squarely upon them, the Soviet leaders finally stopped the charades and cover-ups. In my view, Chernobyl was the catalyst for the collapse of the Soviet Union.

Chernobyl is the quintessential example of how the flawed mind-set of just a few people can ripple out and expand into huge consequences.

The Science of Happy

How happy are you? That is a question we can all ask ourselves. On a scale of one to ten, with one being miserable and ten being very happy, wealthy people typically rate themselves from seven to nine.

Throughout the years, I have been asking this same question of the homeless who attend my class. Surprisingly, the homeless rate themselves from six to nine, about the same as someone who is wealthy. At first, I found this to be astounding, but it is clear that lasting happiness does not come from the things we might have guessed.

One ritual might be to list those things that really make you happy, and then simply deciding to do more of them. It might be as simple as reading a book, going on a hike, or hanging out with certain friends or playing catch with your child. It might be golf, travel, or indulging in pedicures or manicures. Some of these activities might cost money, while others don't; however, having seen many of these lists, I have noted that often those things that bring the most happiness don't cost a dime.

Science has established that money, power, and prestige do not bring authentic happiness.[25] These things yield only temporary spikes above the baseline level. Just look at the faces of people waiting in line for a roller coaster. Some are yelling at their children. Some look happy and some look bored. During the ride, everyone gets a thrill. However, within a few minutes after the ride, they are back to their baseline. Some go back to yelling at their children, laughing, or just being bored.

This simple observation reconciles with science. In a 1978 study, the happiness level of lottery winners was compared to those who had been through a tragedy that left them in a wheelchair. The study showed that money and glory generated temporary spikes of thrills, but soon people typically returned to their baseline level of happiness. On the other hand, those who had suffered a life-altering injury tend to have a temporary downward spike, but they also returned to their baseline level of happiness.[26] In some cases, they may be even happier!

The pursuit of happiness should focus on elevating our baseline, not just grabbing more temporary thrills. This means that if we enjoy more of those habits, rituals, and routines, we will actually raise our baseline level of happiness. To accomplish this, we must understand the complete picture of happiness, which includes 1) our natural brain physiology, 2) our circumstances, and 3) the habits, rituals, and routines we choose.

Historically, the field of psychology focused on mental illnesses and personality disorders. Then a fundamental breakthrough came with a movement led by Dr. Martin Seligman. A group of psychologists started focusing on the science of happiness or "positive psychology." One of the most groundbreaking discoveries within this new field is that happiness has a 50-10-40 ratio, where 50 percent is attributable to our individual DNA, 10 percent for our circumstances, and 40 percent is based upon our activities, habits, rituals, and routines.[27] This study concludes that our inherited DNA explains about 50 percent of happiness.

Our brains have about one hundred billion neurons or neurotransmitters that are responsible for feelings of well-being and happiness. These cells naturally secrete dopamine, norepinephrine, and serotonin, giving us natural highs and lows. This explains, in part, why some people tend to be naturally happy while others are not. In an effort to get more of those highs, some resort to counterfeit highs, such as drugs, overeating, or alcohol to get more of those brain secretions. At first, they do get the thrill. The problem is that they need more and more counterfeit highs to maintain those thrills. On the other hand, authentic highs are much different. Authentic highs do not produce a crash or any kind of depression.

If we inherited poor DNA brain chemistry, then sensible prescription drug therapies can be a solution; however, physical exercise can often reduce or eliminate the dosages.[28]

Our circumstances account for about 10 percent of our happiness. Some circumstances we choose and others we do not. In other words, being disabled accounts for only 10 percent of one's level of happiness. Likewise, being wildly rich or famous accounts for only 10 percent of one's happiness. That is why so many celebrities and trust-fund kids end up in drug rehabilitation. It is a myth that materialism or fame generates authentic, lasting happiness.

A full 40 percent of what brings authentic happiness is dependent upon the activities and rituals we choose. This is critical to understand because these are the things of which we have complete control. We have less power of our DNA or circumstances, but we have total control of our activities and attitudes. Indeed, the spectrum of *Me We Do Be* habits includes routines that anyone can engage in. It is simply up to us.

This science explains why most of my homeless students, who are actively rebuilding their lives, regularly report that they are happy. Homelessness itself is a circumstance that accounts for only 10 percent of happiness. Homeless people who are on a solid track of recovery are generally happy for the same reasons that anyone is happy—they are grateful for what they do have, they have a game plan to elevate, and they appreciate that they are a part of a community that cares. They are working hard to keep their minds illuminated, run with the winners, do their daily chores and rituals, and set goals for the future.

In large part, happiness is simply a choice. Misery may not be a conscientious choice, but by not doing anything about it, it does become a choice. The secret of happiness is to choose to be happy.

Passion Pays Big Dividends

At one time, scientists and doctors said it was anatomically impossible for a human being to run a mile in less than four minutes. Then, an optimist by the name of Roger Banister came along and did it. A lot of people know this, but what is less known is that the four-minute mile was broken again just a few weeks later, and then again and again.

The record had to be broken mentally first, and then it was broken physically by scores of people.

Some people have such amazing passion that they are a remarkable source of inspiration. More than four hundred banks and investors rejected Walt Disney's theme park idea, but he kept going. I have a Michael Jordan autographed basketball on my shelf. When my children complain about some setback, I point at the ball and remind them that Jordan was cut from his high school basketball team. Obviously, he didn't let that setback get in his way. Most people know that Babe Ruth set a home run world record, but that great Yankee also set strikeout records as well. On top of that, Babe Ruth was not an orphan as often thought. It was worse than that. His mother and father, while both alive and together, placed him into an orphanage. Yet, he overcame all of that. Scientists told the athlete Carl Lewis that it was physically impossible for a human to jump more than thirty feet, yet he did it. Oprah Winfrey was born to an unwed, fourteen-year-old mother, but went on to become a media mogul and billionaire.

Each of these people persisted. There must be some risk, some fire, and some passion. The one who goes farthest is the one who is willing to take a risk. Helen Keller said, "Security is mostly a superstition. Life is either a daring adventure or it is nothing." One can never become what he or she wants to become by remaining where he or she is. Every one of these people had an elevated mind-set.

The *Me* habits are those things that elevate our core thinking. Our thoughts, feelings, and beliefs fuel our passion. The *Me* habits are important because they create the illumination that sets us in the direction we will go.

Chapter 3

Philosophical

Stand for Something

Get a Buzz

We all have neurotransmitters in our brains and we all need endorphins, those powerful chemicals that surge through our veins and make us feel great.[29] While we all need them, the question is, "Where do we get them?" This is critical because there are both good and bad ways to get buzzed.

Neurotransmitters can be stimulated by anger, becoming upset, or feeling terrorized. Many people become addicted to these negative stimulations. Perhaps one of the more common examples would be watching a horror movie. But even the daily news can generate this negative buzz. News agencies know that if they report everyday events or even good news, their ratings go flat. But if they sensationalize problems, dig out gossip, and manufacture controversy,

> ### Rich Habit #2
> ### Just Let It Go
>
> An angry temperament was studied as a function of those who tend to yell at bad drivers. Those who just let it go tend to be more than two times happier and wealthier. compared to those who don't.

they generate a negative buzz and get more viewers. Many people become news junkies. This can elevate into an actual need to feel rage or a broader problem of anger addiction.[30] Being addicted to anger is a relatively common phenomenon that can destroy lives and relationships.

There is good and there is evil and we need to know the difference.

Habits generate a buzz. Are we going to get our buzz through habits of anger, greed, cheap highs, worry, fault-finding, violence, rage, stealing, hate, loveless sex, criticism, over-eating, binge-shopping, using illegal drugs, or gambling? Or perhaps worse, are we going to get our buzz from self-righteous delusions, gossip, manufacturing drama, hypocrisy, narcissism, or abusing a position we hold over others?

Or, are we going to thrive and get our buzz through a healthy lifestyle, exercise, love, romance, laughter, art, spirituality, relaxation, learning, music, good foods, family, friendships, faith, service, generosity, and kindness?

Many of the homeless people I teach have addiction problems. I tell them to go get buzzed. Get a runner's high, get spiritually high, read a book and get brain buzzed, or do something for someone else and get a helper's high.[31] I tell them to get high on life, but to shun everything that produces a counterfeit high.

Why is it important to reflect on what habits give us a buzz? The reason is that, in the end, we become what we think about. The *Me* habits are the chief cornerstone that distinguishes between those who are just living day to day, consumed by meaningless or toxic behaviors, and those who elevate to a life of meaning.

The *Me* habits are those principles where one fundamentally chooses between light and dark alternatives. These choices are important. While all *Me* habits are a solo exercise, these key choices create one's own energy that then attracts like-minded people into one's life.

Quality Thinking

In a study published in 1987, researchers asked participants to not think about a white bear for five minutes.[32] The participants were told to ring a bell every time they thought about a white bear. The participants were then asked to *be sure* to think about a white bear for five minutes. They were likewise asked to ring a bell every time they did.

Remarkably, the participants who tried to suppress their thoughts rang the bell almost twice as often as those who were explicitly told to think of a white bear. It appears that trying to suppress thoughts make people fight back all the stronger. If you don't believe me, go up to a child, hand him or her a raisin and tell the child to not stick it in his nose; then watch where he sticks it. This also works on some adults!

The White Bear study shows that it is difficult to suppress thoughts. We have a choice in how we think, and there are measureable consequences from those choices.

As the old adage goes, "We must be careful of what stick we pick up, as we always pick up the other end too." We can pick a choice, but we cannot pick the consequence. We might ask, "Is this habit of thinking dragging me down or lifting me up?" Life is too short to be lived small. We must take control. We must own our mind-set and take responsibility for the way we think.

> **Rich Habit #3**
> **Don't Sweat It**
>
> In a word frequency analysis, when asked about bad habits, "worrying too much" ranked number one worst *Me* habit.

Often our thinking comes down to two choices. I love the story about the elderly Cherokee's lesson to his grandson. The chief explains that there are two wolves inside us, and they are in a battle. One is kind, loving, intelligent, forgiving, and full of joy. The other is full of darkness, ignorance, hate, and envy.

The grandson thinks about this for a while, and then asks his grandfather, "Grandpa, which wolf wins?" to which the wise, great chief replies, "The one you feed."

If we have taken the wrong path, then we need to change.[33] Albert Einstein said, "Insanity is doing the same thing over and over again and expecting different results." We cannot expect different results when we remain on the same path. Sometimes we need to slam on the brakes and turn around. We need to reboot. We need to call a time out. In other words, to change directions we must deliberately develop new, good habits.

My family once remodeled a home. We have spent small fortunes moving walls, replacing doors and windows, and putting in new sinks and cabinets. It often occurred to me that we were ripping out perfectly good materials because of a poor design. It costs about the same to construct a bad design as a good one, so it is critical to have a well-designed plan in the first place.

The *Me* habits are really design concepts, where we conscientiously reflect upon and design our destiny. The better the design in the first place, the less likely we will have to tear things apart and rebuild later.

Attitude

Winston Churchill said, "A pessimist sees the difficulty in every opportunity; an optimist sees the opportunity in every difficulty."

Nobody likes it, but disappointments hit everyone at one time or another. They hit me and they hit you. Failures should be expected and accepted. It could be any one of what I call the "Difficult D's" such as disease, death, divorce, disability, drugs, defeat, or being dumped. Sometimes people cause their own disappointments while others just get it handed to them.

When we fail, we should fail forward. While disappointments are inevitable, my focus is on what I call "post-traumatic thrivers." These are people who are resilient and actually come out stronger than before. They do it deliberately and make some key choices.

First, post-traumatic thrivers accept challenges. They do not operate under the delusion that they are entitled to a life of continual bliss. They have a continual sense of gratitude for what they have and gravitate toward the positive.[34] They tend to be inclusive and fun. On the other hand, when the challenges come, they handle them constructively and with dignity. They reject blame and take responsibility.

When the Difficult D's come, it is understandable to get upset, cry, shut down, or even go into a rage, but post-traumatic thrivers do not become bitter. Bitterness means never letting go. It is the poison that signifies total defeat. On the other hand, post-traumatic thrivers don't just go forward, they go upward.

Post-traumatic thrivers tend to have faith in a higher power. Many people are riding on the momentum on the faith of their parents or grandparents. Recommitting to our own spiritual journey, however we define it, is a core ingredient to thriving. This is especially true when life comes at you hard.

Our attitude, not aptitude, determines our altitude.[35] We can never change the past, we may not be able to change others, but we have total control of our attitude. Attitude will always beat out facts, education, environment, skill, age, appearance, talent, or money. We cannot always choose our circumstances, but we can always choose our attitude.

Left Line, Right Line

I'm one of those guys who likes his cars and watches. Once I had a beautiful silver convertible sports car with a black, leather interior. It was remarkably fast and the steering was awesome. I have a lot of good memories with that car. On weekends, we would take it for Sunday drives up a canyon near our home.

At times I would be traveling or get busy and not drive the car for several weeks. Then, I would go to take it for a drive and find out the battery was dead. I recall the sense of disappointment when I realized that I had neglected my "little baby." Instead of going on a fun ride, I had to sit around waiting for the tow truck to come and jumpstart my car.

One night, when he was in high school, my son asked me to take the car out and I said, "Sure."

Later that night, I got a call from him saying that he'd had an accident. I was relieved that he was calling me, which meant he was okay. I quickly drove up the canyon and found him and a policeman. My favorite car was wrapped around a massive oak tree.

It was nothing short of a miracle that he was alive. He had been driving more than one hundred miles per hour on the unlit, twisting canyon road in the rain. He had lost control, spun out, and hit a fence and then went into the tree. The fence reduced his speed and saved his life. Later, the insurance adjuster said that he had never seen a car so totaled in his career.

"Left line, right line" is a concept I developed to identify human behaviors. Summed up, left line negligence, and right line extremes often determine our bottom line results.

When I forgot about my car and the battery died, that was due to my left line negligence. When my son drove the car too fast and lost control, that was right line excess.

This concept is important as I work on crises and disasters, as one of the first things I identify are the left line or right line behaviors that caused the problem.

As we access our lives, businesses, and organizations, it can be useful to look at those areas where we have been left line negligent or right line excessive. Often, when we think of our habits, we might focus on where we have been negligent. However, right line excess can often be more damaging.

It is good to be principled, but it is right line behavior when we try and force our own values on others. It is great to exercise, but it is right line when we go too far and injure ourselves. It is great to earn a profit, but it is right line when we neglect our family and loved ones to do it.

Right line excess resulted in my dream car being totaled, and right line actions often cause great destruction. For brief periods we might get away with being a little lax or pushing exceptionally hard, but overall we must operate between the right line and left line.

A Mission

To achieve anything, we must have a strategy.[36] When I walk into a boardroom in New York City to consult on the World Trade Center attack, drive through the devastated streets of New Orleans after Hurricane Katrina, or cut through the jungle of the Bikini Atoll nuclear weapons test sites, I have a clear strategic plan in place. I have to. Billions of dollars are riding on those decisions.

The four cornerstones of *Me We Do Be* are assessment tools that prompt us to stop, look and listen and think about what is important to us, what is not, and where we want to go. Our bottom line results are ultimately the consequence of our mind-set. A noble mind-set and a clear purpose will send us on an upward direction and ultimately lead to high achievement, while an undisciplined mind-set and an unclear purpose will ultimately yield to the powers of gravity and result in chaos and failure.

Albert Einstein once said, "The significant problems we face cannot be solved at the same level of thinking we were at when we created them." If we are truly interested in elevating, we must pause once in a while, examine past setbacks, look at what worked and what didn't, and be willing to adopt—and act on—a more effective mind-set.

A sense of purpose, coupled with clarity and core values, is a powerful mix that ignites passion and results in a deeply satisfying path. This concept has value for business management, real estate management, crisis management, and household management.

This does not mean that a person with a clear purpose and core values will not stumble along the way. Setbacks are inevitable. But people traveling with strong core values know that problems are just opportunities in disguise and see setbacks as valuable lessons. While sure of their mission, they are always open to learning more and improving on the past.

Our purpose, good, bad, or indifferent, sends us in the direction we will go. A clear purpose is what drives one to an upward path and draws others in. A person or organization with a clear agenda that is based upon sound core values and principles will grow and flourish.[37] They know why they are there and what needs to be done.

Digital Drugs

The *Me* habits bring mental illumination and wisdom, but the enemy of illumination is distraction. Today we have an epidemic of what I call "digital drugs." There is no end to smartphones, video games, and computers. As a parent, I spend considerable time fighting these addictions with my children and even myself. Don't be fooled, digital drugs produce neurotransmitters, such as endorphins and dopamine, which are as addictive as morphine. Video games generate endorphins that bring about a feeling of well-being and excitement. Dopamine brings a sense of reward, a similar high to that which comes from cocaine.[39]

We have watched the remarkable evolution of technology throughout the last few decades. When I was in elementary school in the 1960s, we did all of our long division by hand. I remember the night that my dad brought home a hand held calculator. As a family we were amazed and played with it for hours. I quickly figured out that I was able to do an hour's worth of homework in about two minutes. I no longer had to think, and that was the problem.

My dad gave me permission to take the calculator to school for the day and I showed it to my teacher. Nobody in the class had ever seen one before, and it grabbed everyone's attention. That was a turning point. From that point calculators flooded the market. Then it was computers and smartphones.

While Alexander Graham Bell invented the telephone, he refused to have one in his study. He was afraid that a phone would distract him from his scientific work. Imagine what Alexander Bell's reaction would be today, where teenagers go psycho if their cell phone battery goes dead for a few minutes. Technology is awesome and continues to improve our quality of life; however, we need to be careful in a world where there are many deliberately engineered "digital drugs."

The *Me* habits are important to students who, in order to be successful, must think clearly. Some students refuse to leave digital drugs alone while they study. While they are reading their book, they are also listening to music, tracking social media, and texting friends. Some students make the better decision by turning off everything and focusing.

The Foundation for Critical Thinking has extensively researched the various levels of thinking and has documented several stages of thought.[40]

The one who thinks at the lowest level is termed the, "Unreflective Thinker."

> ## Rich Habit #4
> ## Chill Out
>
> There are many so-called bad habits that actually do not statistically reconcile with negative outcomes. For example, the amount of time spent watching television does not correlate with most of the benefits measured. Interestingly, the one strong correlation was between the high amounts of television watched by doctorate degree holders. When the brain is actively working, it generates more beta brain waves that are associated with active learning; however, watching television generates more alpha brain waves, which is a relaxed state. Both alpha and beta brain waves have beneficial effects.

Unreflective thinkers are those who are oblivious, who let life happen to them, and who are largely unaware of the role that thinking plays in their lives. The progression to higher levels of thinking is in proportion to our level of reflective thinking.

Christopher Columbus said, "Riches don't make a man rich, they only make him busier." Money, along with careers or technology, can overtake our attention. Those who make it a regular habit to unplug, quietly reflect on priorities, read, adjust attitudes, and think about their goals will see positive, tangible results. This can include reading books that inspire. There may be no better way to start a day than to have the words of the world's greatest men and women firmly in mind; by them we are elevated and their words can set the tone for the rest of the day.

Digital drugs are not the only means of distraction. I once knew a woman who openly stated that she did not enjoy life when things were quiet. She was addicted to constant movement. She thrived on endless activity, noise, chaos, and commotion. If there was not enough noise, she would create it. She had seven children and then adopted more. I love children, but it was clear that she used hers to create the distraction she craved. She had sensational, wild hand gestures that played along with her manufactured and never-ending dramas. Having trouble sleeping, she was an easy target for all things infomercial. Under a thin veneer of superficial charm, her character was sadly shallow.

> ### Rich Habit #5
> ### Read
>
> Reading dramatically correlates with higher education and income, as well as overall happiness. For example, those who read seven or more books per year dominate in all categories of income and net worth. Those who read seven or more books per year are more than 122.0 percent more likely to be millionaires as opposed to those who never read or only read one to three.

Occasionally, I wondered to myself about what misery she was trying to dodge. Later, I learned that she had made some major mistakes earlier in life and her current husband was hiding a life of deceit. Instead of dealing with these issues, she simply coped through noise and distraction. This was not a healthy solution.

Socrates warned his followers, "Beware the barrenness of a busy life." Distraction, in all its forms, kills the very genesis of authenticity.

Multitasking

The concept of multitasking is somewhat of a myth. Physiologically, the brain is incapable of thinking about more than one thing at a time. The best it can do is to switch back and forth really, really quickly.[41] Like any poor habit, multitasking has a ripple effect. For example, if we study while we watch television, we are likely to miss important details and perform poorly on tests, which can ripple out to poor self-esteem and other problems.

Multitasking can also damage relationships. If a couple is having an important conversation and the husband checks a text message, this may irritate the wife who then checks her messages, all leading to a shutdown of communication. The ripple effect does not stop there. Other poor habits, like eating while watching television or working on the computer, can lead to overeating.[42] Other studies show that texting while driving is as dangerous as drunk driving.[43]

The research shows that it is far less stressful, and far more effective, to stay focused on one task at a time. Our productivity increases when we give a task our full attention.

The Magic of Showers

Often we hear someone say, "I got this great idea in the shower this morning!" What is it about showers? Is it the running water? Is it the fragrance from the soap? Is there some magic from shampoo bubbles? What is it about these little tiled stalls that generate some of the greatest thoughts of mankind?

The magic of showers is the absence of distraction. Showers are one of those rare times when there are no phone calls, no Internet, no television, and no texting. If there is magic in the thoughts that come from showers, it is that showers create a virtually ideal setting for reflection and clear thinking.

We want to create more moments of clear, quiet reflection. Reflection takes on different forms in different contexts.

For students, find a spot where you can think and study without disruption. For CEOs, take some quiet time in the morning to review your company mission statements,

> **Rich Habit #6**
> **Get the Big Picture**
>
> Creating time for solitude not only clears your head and brings a higher degree of focus, but solitude correlates with education. Those who seek daily solitude are up to 92.3 percent more likely to have an advanced college degree.

contemplate the big picture, and plan out the day's activities. For teachers, take a moment to think about the students and adjust your lesson plan. For parents, sneak away, read an inspiring book, and reflect on the meaning of raising a family. For anyone, just sit and stare at the ocean, a valley, or a river while thinking about what is important to you.

There have been many poor choices that felt good, but lacked common sense. On the other hand, there have been choices that intellectually were sound, yet had no soul. When we combine intellectual information with spiritual and philosophical insights, we are able to develop wisdom. Critical thinking means that we consider our issues and make choices that are logically sound, reconcile with our core values, and feel right.

Many people know of Albert Einstein's Theory of Relativity and his famous formula, $E=mc^2$. What is less known is how he came to this and other remarkable discoveries.

Einstein's discoveries came as a result of a process he referred to as "gifted isolation." For hours, days, and even weeks, Einstein's routine was to go into seclusion and just think. He was obsessed with finding a formula that explained the science of the universe. Einstein knew that if he was going to reach his objective, he needed to eliminate all distractions and focus entirely upon his own thoughts. These periods of deep, personal reflection are often the starting point of every great pursuit.

Jon Benét Ramsey

Those in the habit of lifelong education thrive, while those who don't, dive.

On December 26, 1997, a six-year-old girl, JonBenét Ramsey, was reported kidnapped from her home in Boulder, Colorado. Her body was later found in the home's basement. The case garnered world-wide attention, as the young girl had been in beauty pageants and speculation ran rampant on who committed this horrible crime. Police initially focused on the parents as potential suspects, but later formally cleared them from suspicion. To this day the crime remains unsolved.

When the Ramseys wanted to sell their home, I was asked to advise the couple on the effect of crime-scene stigma. Before I consulted on the project, I had two conditions: First, I had made some comments about the Ramseys that had been quoted in *The Denver Post*. They needed to be aware of them because they were not complimentary. Second, in lieu of a fee, I asked that a donation be made to the Nicole Brown Charitable Foundation. I had no desire to profit from a crime like this. With those conditions met, I consulted on the case.

During the course of the assignment I heard some comments from those who were involved with the case. Having worked on this case and having talked extensively with people in the district attorney's office, I believe I know who killed JonBenét; however, it cannot ever be proven. The police on the scene did not seal off the scene and they even let more people into the house, so the crime scene was irreparably contaminated. Clearly, the

Rich Habit #7
Get Smart

In a word frequency analysis, having an advanced education ranked as the number one *Me* accomplishment. On the other hand, the lack of an advanced education ranked as the all-time top regret.

Greatest *Me* Accomplishments	Habit Index
College	174
Career	118
Being happy	31

Biggest Regrets	
Lack of college degree	345
People skills	199
Marriage relationship	149
Treatment of family	139
Wasting time	136
Career choices	134
Money management	125
Choice of friends	29
Parent Relationship	27
Not traveling	26

department had given little weight to ongoing training on the topic of crime scene investigations. They failed intellectually by a lack of continuing education.

Success can only come to those who are in the habit of lifelong education. They do their homework. Those on an intellectual quest are generally in the habit of reading books, professional journals, and magazines on their chosen fields of interest. They attend seminars and conferences, as well as listen to podcasts or audiobooks. They take careful notes and do whatever it takes to stay on top of their game.

When Life Comes at You Hard

One day I was walking down the hall in a halfway house where I was volunteering when I saw that someone had taped a paper to the wall. It said, "You don't fail when you lose, you fail when you quit." I stopped and read this over and over. I admit that I got a little choked up as I thought about how these people had the courage to keep going, to face their problems, to endure the pain, and take another step forward.

Some failures are self-induced, while others are more a matter of dumb luck or simply the fate of the genetic lottery we all play. Whatever the source of our difficulties, an effective way of dealing with it is to look at the situation with some perspective. Indeed, with a sense of perspective, we can almost appreciate the difficulties we have been handed.

There is a path along a bluff in Santa Monica, California, that overlooks the ocean. It is close to where I lived when I was in graduate school. Often I would go down and run on this path past a beautiful rose garden. I had the habit of stopping, walking up, and smelling the roses. Literally, I would go from bush to bush and smell them. The scents would vary from color to color. Coupled with the ocean air, it was like taking in a deep breath of heaven.

One day, I bought a bouquet of roses to take home to my wife. On the drive home, I took a deep, deep breath and I got, well, I got nothing. I thought that something was wrong with my sense of smell. I tried again and again, and still no smell.

I came to learn that in today's society of mass production, many roses are grown in "perfect" greenhouse conditions. They face no wind, no harsh sun, no rain, no scorching hot days, and no freezing cold nights. They get the ideal amounts of water and chemical fertilizers. In this perfect world, they grow quickly and outwardly they look perfect. But, the bees never get to pollinate them, so they lose their natural fragrance altogether.

I like the roses that face the harsh elements head on and move forward to rise above it all. They do what roses are supposed to do—they remain authentic, they toughen up, overcome the elements, show their beauty, and give the world a wonderful scent.

Booker T. Washington said, "Success is to be measured not so much by the position that one has reached in life as by the obstacles which he has overcome." We may not enjoy the challenges we face, but we can appreciate the growth that comes with them.

The Stanford Marshmallow Study

Good things come to those who can wait. The Stanford Marshmallow Test involved deferred gratification and was conducted by Dr. Walter Mischel in the early 1970s.[44]

Dr. Mischel put a marshmallow on a plate in front of a four-year-old child. The child was given the choice to eat the marshmallow right then, or if he waited about fifteen minutes until the researcher returned from an errand, he could have another marshmallow. The researchers would secretly watch the child's reaction.

Of all the children tested, about a third of the children immediately shoved the marshmallow into their mouths. About a third waited for a while, but gave in and ate the marshmallow after a few minutes of agony. And finally, about a third of the children waited the full fifteen minutes for the researcher's return and were rewarded with a second marshmallow.

What made this experiment so powerful was that it was a longitude study, meaning that these children were observed over a long period of time. The findings were telling. The children who grabbed the marshmallow right away tended to be more introverted, stubborn, easily upset, jealous, envious, and

> ### Rich Habit #8
> ### Do the Homework
>
> Those with advanced degrees are far more likely to save money and build wealth. Those with a master's degree are about 144 percent more likely to be saving 10 percent of their money as opposed to being in debt and those with a doctorate degree are 319 percent more likely.

argumentative. They tended to be less successful in life. As adults, they were more impulsive and prone to addictive habits and behaviors.

In contrast, those who waited went on to be more socially self-assertive, self-reliant, and confident. They also scored higher on test scores and were more academically successful.

Science has shown that patience is indeed a virtue. The highest levels of achievement are reserved for those who can overcome the urge for immediate gratification and instead see the big picture. Seeing the big picture, they seek a quality education and gradually build something of genuine value.

Reflective people tend to select things of authentic value that don't fade when the crowds, lights, and cheap thrills are gone. The choice in front of us may not be a matter of good versus evil, but of good verses better. Often, we must give up something good for something great.

Always Teachable

After his first day of first grade, my oldest son asked me, "Dad, I really love school. How old do you get when you are done learning?" It's an intriguing question because many people have the attitude that once they are past a certain point, their education is complete. I told my son that someday we may finish high school or college, but we never finish our education.

Continuing education is vital. The vast majority of college graduates end up in a field that has nothing to do with their major.[45] We should always remain on guard against being qualified for a world that no longer exists. Each day, we are faced with new situations that require us to be continuously learning. Aristotle said, "The difference between being educated and uneducated is the same difference as being alive and being dead."

There are a number of relatively simple actions we can take that can keep us informed. As individuals, we might continually ask ourselves, "Am I teachable and actively learning new things?" Our education can always continue through traveling,

> ### Rich Habit #9
> ### Learn to Learn
> Advanced education has measurable benefits. People without a college degree are more likely to earn less than $50,000, while those with a degree dominate in all categories more than $50,000 per year.

trips to museums, reading, and even surfing the Internet. In business, we should regularly ask ourselves, "Are we actively training and learning as a team?" This is accomplished through continuing education, updating our technical and computer skills, and being involved with sales and customer service training. There is only one thing worse than training people and losing them—not training people and keeping them.

Irrespective of one's natural aptitude, a few basic rules can increase our learning. First, the mother of learning is repetition. I learned this principle as a Boy Scout. When I was at a Scout jamboree, we had a class on packing our backpacks. The instructor was covering all kinds of material, none of which I could recount today. Then he said something that stuck.

"Now, *Scouts!*" he shouted. "It is critical to keep the contents of your packs organized! When packing, never, never, never, never, never, never, never, never, never, never, never, never forget to always pack similar items in small plastic bags!"

When I got back to camp, I told our scoutmaster about this strange teacher and how he had repeated himself ten or twelve times. My scoutmaster replied, "Well, you haven't forgotten have you?" I got his point.

Today, I can't remember many of my Boy Scout knots or much of anything else I learned but because of that repetitive phrase, I never forget to use plastic bags when packing a backpack, a habit I have continued today each time I pack my suitcase.

Another simple action is to take notes. When your ear gathers information, it then travels down your spine, through your arm, into your hand, and onto paper. This process greatly increases your absorption of that information.

Sometimes when I am in a meeting or listening to a great speaker, I look around and am amazed that I'm the only one taking notes. If you just sit and listen, your retention is less than 20 percent a few days later. When you take notes, however, your retention at least doubles, even if you never look at your notes again.[46]

If you choose to review your notes, your retention goes up to about

50 percent. If you take notes, and then share the concepts with another person, you effectively become a teacher. Your retention of the material will go up to well over 75 percent. These simple rituals can literally raise your level of intelligence.

To grow intellectually, we must consistently remain teachable. Success can result in arrogance, and arrogance often results in failure. On the other hand, genuine intellect means that we always remain open to learning, being inquisitive, asking critical questions, and even studying the same material repeatedly.

Chapter 5

Spiritual

Connect with a Higher Power

Spiritual Poverty

Frequently I am in places that remind me that millions of people go to bed hungry every night.[47] Many people shudder at the images of people, particularly children, who are stuck in a world of poverty.

When I visited Africa with one of my sons, we were stunned to see the level of poverty firsthand. Yet, I was equally surprised to see all the smiles on the children's faces. Everywhere we drove the children would wave and smile. My son and I were handing out packs of pens and paper to the children when the village chief stopped us. He did not want them to get "spoiled" and felt that one pen per child was enough. The children still went crazy with excitement and gratitude.

> ### Rich Habit #10
> ### Keep the Faith
>
> In a word frequency analysis on goals, people's top responses centered on family, career, health and money. However, the #1 *Me* goal was to, "Get closer to God."

I've seen the same phenomena in parts of Egypt, Mexico, Peru, China, and the remote islands of Malaysia. How could this be? How could these children seem so happy when they wore rags, had little food, and their homes were made out of plywood or sticks?

On the other hand, I have seen children in Beverly Hills, Paris, and posh areas of London who didn't smile much at all. Yes, much of the world lives in financial poverty, at least by Western standards, but it is clear that much of the world lives in something worse, which is spiritual poverty.

Spiritual poverty is a state where individuals have little or no belief in anything bigger than themselves. Of course, not every poor person is spiritually enriched, neither is every wealthy person spiritually inept. There may be no correlation between financial poverty and spiritual poverty; however, spiritual poverty is tragic.

At some level, we all suffer from spiritual poverty. We all fall far short. This is not meant as an excuse, but it is a reality. We all mess up. Some of the wisest words ever spoken were shared by my youngest son who was ten-years-old at the time. I had done something wrong and he said, "Dad, sometimes to be successful, you just have to say you're sorry and that you will do better. It's just that easy."

A lack of humility is a key sign of spiritual poverty. Those in deep

> ### Rich Habit #11
> ### Stay in Tune
>
> Attending church or synagogue generally correlates with higher education. As a percentage, master and doctorate degree holders beat out all other categories as those who regularly worship, 92.4 percent higher than high school graduates.

spiritual poverty tend to see the faults of others very clearly. On the other hand, those who are spiritually rich tend to see their own faults clearly. In fact, they see them so clearly that they don't have time to worry about the other guy's faults. Humility and acknowledging our own issues generates authenticity.

There are some who believe that their failings are superior to someone else's. They actually believe that their sins are of a higher quality, thus they feel superior. These are the self-righteous, one of the most toxic groups. They are harsh, and their judgments and gossip can damage lives and drive people away. They are the hardest to reach. They have indeed mastered the art of self-deception.[48]

The *Me* habits are a direct assault on spiritual poverty. We stop and contemplate upon those things that give life genuine meaning. We open the mental curtains and let the illumination and deeper feeling filter in. We listen to our conscience. We nourish thoughts that elevate us. We get a clearer view of what sets us apart from every other person on the planet. We look toward something greater than ourselves.

Spirituality is something that happens inside of us. Outward signs such as attendance in a church, synagogue, or mosque do not make anyone spiritual any more than sleeping in the garage will turn someone into a Chrysler. But for many people, organized religion profoundly helps them in their spiritual journey.

Attending one's place of worship is only one habit that can inspire.[49] Meditation, prayer, reading scriptures, or other inspiring works, music, and nature walks are all habits that can build our spiritual core. Simple habits of just smiling and laughing can displace the poor habits of being grim or too sarcastic.

Many of society's designs attempt to center our lives on big box outlets and strip malls, accumulating more stuff and focusing on empty notions of entertainment. We are more than this. We are here by intelligent design.

Pascal's Wager

World religions vary, yet they all seem to agree on some significant points. Lives without soul ultimately lead nowhere. Faith is the greatest hope builder of all. People who have faith and who are true to their faith are the better for it. One study showed that people of faith enjoyed a variety of benefits. They tend to be healthier, live longer, and be more content.[50]

When it comes to belief in God, there are basically four options. Theists believe in God, with the possibility of revelation. This would include believers in most world religions. Deists believe that reason and nature alone is evidence of a God, but reject the concept of revelation or the supernatural. Neil Armstrong was a well-known deist. Agnostics question or doubt the existence of God. Atheists deny the existence of any supreme being.

I once had lunch with a well-known celebrity. We exchanged e-mail addresses and his reflected a strong message that he was a devout atheist.

Through our correspondence, he went on to tell me he did not believe in anything that could not be scientifically proven and added, "If something requires faith, you can count me out." I told him that atheism is an interesting theory, but it hardly rises to the level of scientific fact. One cannot scientifically prove that no God exists until one searches the universe and verifies that no God exists anywhere. He was annoyed with my observation that, like it or not, by embracing atheism he had faith, and he put his faith in an unproven theory.

Believers have faith. Some atheists discredit faith, but the logical fallacy is that it requires considerable faith to be an atheist. I do not have the faith required to be an atheist. To be an atheist, you must have complete faith in an unproven theory that cannot be scientifically proven, and you must ignore all the evidence of intelligent design. In the words of the legendary musician Carlos Santana, "You are free to believe in nothing, and that's exactly what you'll get!" No matter how people define their personal philosophies, faith in something is required. Faith is an inevitable aspect of life. We are merely faced with a choice of where to put it.

One of the most powerful arguments for the existence of God was made by the seventh century French philosopher and mathematician, Blaise Pascal. Called "Pascal's Wager," the logic is that people bet with their lives on the existence or non-existence of God.[51]

Given the possibility that God does actually exist, and living a kind life accordingly, one stands to benefit for eternity. Thus, Pascal would argue that a rational person would live as though God does exist and would endeavor to nurture that belief in God. The logic continues that if God actually does not exist, one would only forego some temporary luxuries or other taboo pleasures of limited worth.

As a mathematician, Pascal considered the odds and concluded that given what is at stake, betting on God's existence outweighs any benefits of atheism.

A Good Thing Too Far

Mark Twain tells about a church sermon he heard. It was so inspiring that he wanted to put all of his money in the collection plate. But the preacher just kept on going, pounding away at his pulpit, and eventually Mark Twain felt like putting *some* of his money in the plate. As the sermon continued, he decided to not put any money in the plate. By the time the preacher finished, Twain took some money out of the plate![52]

While a good, spiritual mind-set is essential, too much of a good thing can be damaging. Going overboard is just as dangerous as being unprincipled. A mind-set that is harsh, inflexible, or excessive is simply out of balance. Fanatics exist in businesses, families, religions, clubs, neighborhoods, and politics; these individuals are compelled to push their ideas onto others.

It is good to stand for something. However, while offering suggestions, ideas, or beliefs to others can be thoughtful, others have the right to say no or disagree. Freedom and critical thinking is essential. The passionate person will pursue his or her objectives while respecting the rights of others. The fanatic will pursue his or her objectives at any cost.

The Good Samaritan Study

In one of the most revealing human behavioral studies, theology students were tested in regard to how their professed beliefs reconciled with their actions.[53] The students were told that they were participating in a study about religious education by reading the story of the Good Samaritan.

In this classic biblical parable, a man taking a journey is beaten, robbed, and left for dead. One priest passes by him and then another. Then comes a Samaritan, a born enemy, who stops, renders aid, and takes the man to an inn to recover. The Good Samaritan even pays for everything.

The students reviewed the full story and filled out a personality questionnaire. They were then told to prepare a speech about the Good Samaritan and present it in a nearby room. On their way to give their presentation, they walked down a hall where a man, an actor, had tripped and had dropped all of his papers. The man appeared to be hurt and clearly needed help. Remarkably only 40 percent of the theology students who were in route to give a speech on the Good Samaritan actually stopped to be a Good Samaritan. Seriously, 60 percent of those who had dedicated their lives and careers to ministry literally stepped over a guy who had fallen and been hurt on their way to delivering a speech on being a Good Samaritan.

People may intellectually know the right thing to do, but not actually do it. The 60 percent who rushed by professed one thing yet actually did another. The 60 percent of these theological students failed this test for the same reason that many people do. They lacked integrity when it came to aligning their desired public image and their actual core beliefs.

When I work on a disaster, the first step is to fully assess the situation and gather information. In this phase, I have little to say, but I do ask a lot of questions. An honest assessment is a universal requirement for recovery. The highest levels of achievement can only occur when we assess what we honestly believe, think, and feel. We must insure that these three elements are in alignment.

The point of the Good Samaritan study is not to point a judgmental finger at these theological students. The point of this study is to take a look at ourselves. Everyone has "onstage" and "backstage" behavior. We put on our onstage public performances with what we want people to think, whereas backstage is how we really are. The students who failed the Good Samaritan study went onstage with an image of becoming ministers, but backstage they really had a limited interest in the beliefs they professed.

The reason *Me* habits are critical is that we can only make our own assessment by turning off all distractions and contemplating our true core beliefs. We must critically assess if our backstage thinking is genuinely in line with our onstage behaviors. We must identify those areas where we have mastered the art of self-deception and resolve to take action with new *Me* habits.

A set of authentic *Me* habits can elevate us to a point where we are aligned with the 40 percent of the students who passed the test—who stopping in the hallway and helped a person in need.

To successfully elevate, what we profess must materialize in how we actually behave.

Chapter 6
The Next Step for *Me*

Lessons from Great Lives

E very great pursuit was solidly built upon *Me* habits. When we look at the personal habits of great historic figures, we inevitably see examples of people who spent considerable time in solitude and deep thought.

Leonardo da Vinci spent remarkable amounts of time in self-imposed isolation pondering universal truths, studying science, or observing nature. Often, he would lock himself away in a workshop and hide. As his fame rose, there was a period of years when nobody had any account of his whereabouts whatsoever.

While World War II was raging, Winston Churchill usually did not show up at the War Cabinet headquarters until after lunchtime. He spent the mornings in the *Me* habit of solitude, reading, studying, and thinking about the developments in the war. Churchill actually came to many key, strategic decisions while sitting in bed. This unconventional routine allowed Churchill to absorb, think, and reflect upon the progress of the war in the quiet of his quarters.

Harry Houdini was far more than a magician and escape artist. He had a pure zest for life. Houdini starred in several motion pictures, wrote seven books, consulted with several police departments, and was

---

Rich Habit #12

Know Thyself

Meditation or prayer correlates with a variety of benefits. Those who meditate or pray daily are 51.8 percent more likely to be happy.

---

the first person to fly a plane on the continent of Australia. His pride and joy was a very large library on the top floor of his home in New York. He would regularly seclude himself and spend hours at a time reading, studying, and thinking.

My childhood home sat on a hill where on hot summer nights we would rush out and sit on the porch to watch the fireworks at Disneyland. Walt Disney, whose genius lead to one of the world's greatest entertainment empires, was a reflective man and had the habit of prayer. He said,

> *I am personally thankful that my parents taught me at a very early age to have a strong personal belief and reliance in the power of prayer for Divine inspiration. My people were members of the Congregational Church in our home town of Marceline, Missouri. It was there where I was first taught the efficacy of religion... how it helps us immeasurably to meet the trial and stress of life and keeps us attuned to the Divine inspiration... Deeds rather than words express my concept of the part religion should play in everyday life. I have watched constantly that in our movie work the highest moral and spiritual standards are upheld, whether it deals with fable or with stories of living action.*

> *This religious concern for the form and content of our films goes back forty years to the rugged financial period in Kansas City when I was struggling to establish a film company and produce animated fairy tales. Many times during those difficult years... we were under pressure to sell out or debase the subject matter or go "commercial" in one way or another. But we stuck it out*

> *Both my study of Scripture and my career in entertaining children have taught me to cherish them... Thus, whatever success I have had in bringing clean, informative entertainment to people of all ages, I attribute in great part to my Congregational upbringing and my lifelong habit of prayer.*

Walt Disney's connection to his faith-based community and his efforts to connect with a higher power, afforded him the insights and directions to meet his high objectives.

This is the same perspective shared by all of history's spiritual, philosophical, and religious figures who regularly had the routine of personal isolation and reflection.

When he was weighed down with questions, Moses went alone to the top of Mount Sinai. Jesus of Nazareth prepared for His ministry by going into the wilderness in complete solitude for forty days and forty nights.

Buddha spent considerable time in meditation and told his followers that peace comes from within, and that our worst enemy cannot harm us as much as our own thoughts, unguarded. He said, "To enjoy good health, to bring true happiness to one's family, to bring peace to all, one must first discipline and control one's own mind. If a man can control his mind he can find the way to Enlightenment, and all wisdom and virtue will naturally come to him."

Socrates advised, "Wisdom begins in wonder. Employ your time in improving yourself by other men's writings, so that you shall gain easily what others have labored hard for." Plato said, "We can easily forgive a child who is afraid of the dark; the real tragedy of life is when men are afraid of the light." Aristotle proclaimed that "Happiness depends upon ourselves. The ultimate value of life depends upon awareness and the power of contemplation rather than upon mere survival."

Quiet Time

I tend to naturally wake up early. As I travel so much, I usually wake up dazed and confused, so my first thoughts are trying to remember what city or country I am in. There is always a great sense of relief when I wake up in my own house!

Like a lot of people, on waking in the morning, my mind immediately starts to flood with thoughts of a busy schedule. There is a temptation to mentally just jump right into the business of the day. Before I go there, I stop to think about my priorities. If I forget, I have even programmed my smartphone to give me a daily reminder to mentally put on the brakes.

For children, "quiet time" can be considered a horribly harsh punishment. They actually have to sit down and be silent for a few minutes! What is agony for them is sheer pleasure to me.

The early morning is the ideal time for me to think about what matters most. I am fully rested. I am fresh and alert. At that point, my mind is relatively uncluttered from the distractions that accumulate throughout the day. Usually I am the first one up, so it is very quiet and I can clearly focus. As I think about my top priorities and purpose, I always take time to read something inspirational. This personal quiet time is my cornerstone *Me* habit. However, this book is not about me, it is about you.

Everyone has morning and evening rituals. They may be to sleep in and drag out of bed and then mindlessly just going to work. At night, the ritual may be to just watch television until we fall asleep. On the other hand, others may get up promptly at a set time and go running, shower, and plan out their day. At night, some might have a vitamin

> **Rich Habit #13**
> **Get Inspired**
> Those who regularly read inspirational works are up to 14.1 percent more likely to be happy

regimen and reflect on the day, then write in their journals. There are many options for morning and evening rituals that range from the sloppy to being more thoughtful. Stepping up and creating more productive morning and evening rituals is essential to grow.

Strategy 360

When a firefighter or other first responder arrives at the scene of a crisis, they usually do not run, they walk. One might wonder why a first responder would walk when there is a serious problem. The reason is that they are looking around as they walk and assessing the full situation, not just running blindly into it.

This first step of assessment is essential in any situation where we hope to elevate. In my consulting work, we often have an exercise that I call "Strategy 360." This is where we simply evaluate our entire situation. In other words, we make a full, honest, and complete assessment of everything we are involved with. Metaphorically, we climb to the top of a mountain and look over the complete landscape as we turn around and look around in all directions.

The first cornerstone is constructed with *Me* habits. It has a survey marker driven into it from which all measurements of the building are referenced. This first step is where we examine our mission, core values, intellectual property, feelings, and beliefs.

These *Me* habits and disciplines are our own responsibility. This task cannot be successfully delegated or assigned to someone else. Each person must create his or her own life vision.

For any great pursuit, it is essential to establish our own point of beginning. These core habits set the benchmark for the entire construction of our lives. Our achievements cannot exceed the level of our thinking and comprehension. There is advanced knowledge already inside of us, but we will never know it unless we regularly turn off all the noise, listen, study, and learn. This is not only the first cornerstone, but it is the *chief cornerstone.*

Our entire life, good, bad, or indifferent, is grounded by this chief cornerstone. Our thoughts become feelings, and our feelings become words. Our words become actions. Our actions bring consequences, and consequences add new thoughts and feelings. These then redefine our core values. They are all inseparably related. If you want to see your future, look where your mind habitually goes when it wanders.

It is not the biggest or strongest who survive, but those who are adaptable to change.[54]   Lives committed to positive change have meaning, while tentative, unprincipled, and cynical lives tend to offer little value. The achiever tends to avoid the term failure. It is not a big part of his or her mind-set. Achievers prefer the term setback. The terms success and failure imply a final point of destination.

My observations show that the final arrival of a person or organization is a myth, because there is always more to come. Setbacks are inevitable. Many wise and great people were once insolent and foolish, but they learned from it. Achievers reserve the right to make mistakes. Problems, mistakes, and even disasters do not necessarily break a person; they simply reveal who the person really is. An achiever knows to take responsibility for any outcome because excuses are fatal to achievement. Achievement is not measured by a single act. Achievement is measured by the trend over time.

Our *Me* habits are entirely up to us. Some people just sit and think. Others read, go running, or take a walk. Some sit or work in their garden or childhood playground. Some create vision boards with pictures of what they want their future to look like. Some use a self-talk technique where they look in the mirror while verbally affirming their personal mission statements. Some do yoga. Others study hard and review their notes. Some do quiet hobbies or construction projects. Some record a statement defining their personal mission, and then listen to it. Many pray and meditate. Some do a combination of these things. The key is to take time away from distractions, clear our minds, adjust our attitudes, and really listen to ourselves.

Happiness is only possible when our core beliefs, thoughts, feelings, and actions are all in alignment. The *Me* habits are important because they facilitate this alignment. While defining our personal vision is essential and even the first step of any great pursuit, it was Thomas Edison who said, "Vision without execution is hallucination."

Furthermore, a building has *four cornerstones*, so what are the other three?

The *Me* Challenge Coin

This is where you accept the challenge coin and take responsibility for your own *Me* cornerstone. This is where you do something to build wisdom, specifically by continually learning, standing for something, and connecting to a higher power.

Avoid the January 4th effect, instead, pick only one new *Me* habit and make it simple. For example, don't commit to reading one hour a week. Rather, commit to reading five minutes a day, but then read more if you choose to.

Commit to mastering your new Me habit and make it a solid cornerstone of your life. Here are some suggestions, or come up with one of your own:

- Write down an ethical standard and follow it.
  (For example, kindness, generosity, integrity, and so on.)
- Completely turn off all technology for _____ minutes a day.
  (For example, Television, Internet, video games, cell phone, and so on.)
- Read for _____ hours every week in your chosen area.
- Create a vision board with pictures of your future.
- Take notes when listening to a presentation.
- Make flash cards of important knowledge and review them repeatedly.
- Enroll in a course at the local community college.
- When a negative thought comes, think of something positive.
- Meditate for _____ minutes every day.
- Write down a personal mission statement that defines who you are, and recite it every morning
- Practice yoga.
- Pray for _____ minutes every day.
- Review your company's mission statement _____ times per week.
- Attend your place of worship _____ times every month.
- Spend _____ hours outdoors every week and connect with nature.
- Write in a "gratitude" journal every night.
- Read _____ minutes of an inspirational work every day.
- Complete every homework assignment on time.
- Turn off all Internet and phone access while studying.
- Study for _____ hours every week night.

SECTION 2
THE *WE* CORNERSTONE

Relationships are the true measure value

Chapter 7
The *We* Habits

Go Blue!

One of my first discoveries of group dynamics occurred when, as a teenager, I went to a jousting tournament with a bunch of friends. Upon arrival, we were each given a blue band to put on our arm and seated for dinner in the blue section. We soon realized that the horses and jousters wore colors that corresponded to all the groups within the giant hall.

Quickly we fell into line and went crazy cheering for our group's horse. What was remarkable was that we knew absolutely nothing about our rider or his horse. Even still, we yelled and screamed for our blue team to win. We chided, jeered, and threw dinner rolls at our red, green, and yellow rivals.

> ### The *We* Cornerstone
>
> The second cornerstone, *We*, is our connection with others. It is the sum of those in our relationships.
>
> To construct this cornerstone, be kind, listen carefully, and communicate effectively. Avoid toxic people and groups, and gravitate toward people of character.

Afterward, I was amazed just how quickly and fanatically our group of total strangers rallied around each other to support our horse and rider. The whole event was so artificial, and yet the group's insane passion was so real.

Group dynamics have been carefully studied by social scientists. One behavior study referred to as the *Robber's Cave Study,* assigned two groups of boys to camp out for an extended period of time.[55] At first, the two groups of boys were unaware of the other group's existence.

Detailed observations were made of the group's dynamics. The two groups had predictable behaviors of establishing a name, seeking a leader, establishing rituals and rules, and patriotism. When the two groups were introduced to each other, they were immediately competitive and each had spontaneous, unjustified feelings of superiority over the other.

These observations and group studies led to many questions. What draws us to the groups we are in? Why this group? What does this group do for me? Is this the right group? How do I contribute to the group? Would it be better to be open-minded and explore other groups? Should I remain with the group I am in, but maybe be a little more tolerant of others?

Ex caritas is Latin for *of kindness, love, and gratitude*. With the *Me* habits, discussed in the previous section, we develop disciplines to elevate our individual sense of purpose and mental illumination. But with *ex caritas* and *We* habits, we shift from being *Me* focused to focusing on *We*—the people around us. This could be summed up as connection. Upon this cornerstone, we connect with others and we post the flag for our affiliations. Connection and connecting with the right people is the essence of the *We* habits.

Durham Woods

Durham Woods is a thousand-unit apartment complex located in Edison, New Jersey. Near midnight, on March 23, 1994, an underground, high-pressure, methane gas pipeline exploded near the complex.

The explosion created a crater sixty feet deep and sent a three-hundred-foot fireball into the air that could be seen by residents of New Jersey, New York, and Pennsylvania. The event was so disastrous that it was designated a federal disaster area.

While the fire burned out of control, it took workers nearly three hours to turn off the gas flow, which they eventually accomplished by turning a valve one small turn at a time. The apartment's 1,500 tenants were forced to flee their homes in the middle of the night. A total of 128 apartments were completely destroyed. The next morning, a team of police officers conducted the grim task of searching for bodies.

When I consulted on this case, I toured the area that had been incinerated.

The fire had burned so hot that it literally melted the red lights on the fire trucks and charred trees that were hundreds of yards away. Cars that had been parked in the apartment complex's parking lot had melted into liquid pools of metal.

> ### Rich Habit #14
> ### Be Kind
>
> Those who tend to smile and speak positively are 43.5 percent more likely to be happy. If that doesn't cut it, they are also up to 46 percent more likely to be millionaires.

The apartment buildings themselves were burned right down to their foundations and no framing remained. I asked the owners of the development how many people had died. I was stunned yet happy to learn that no lives had been lost. Even though the tragedy occurred near midnight, all of the 1,500 victims successfully escaped.

How could this have been possible? The answer was simple. The neighborhood was full of people who had developed solid, supportive relationships with each other. When the explosion woke up some people, they took the time to bang on doors to wake up all their neighbors before fleeing for their lives. Certainly, without this reaction, dozens or even hundreds of people would have been killed. These strong *We* habits and friendships not only create a spirit of community support, but in this case literally saved lives. *We* habits are all the things we do to build relationships, nurture friendships, and connect with the people in our lives.

Elevate Your Team

Social Capital

Social capital is a term that behavioral scientists use to describe one's level of connection, respect, or clout that has been built up within a group to which one belongs.[56] This is something that can be far more valuable than financial capital.

Once I had dinner at the home of one of Hollywood's top movie producers. Two famous movie stars called while I was there. This guy had the social capital to be able to put together a major motion picture whenever he wanted. People with social capital know whom to call to get things done. A well-connected politician, executive, or leader could have enough social capital to put together a major deal with just a few phone calls.

There are two types of social capital: earned and unearned. Earned social capital comes through intelligence, hard work, and effort. Einstein, Lincoln, and Edison all earned their social capital. On the other hand, trust-fund-kids or royalty are examples of those who have unearned social capital. Beethoven was blunt about it when

> **Rich Habit #15**
>
> **Remember Birthdays**
>
> Those who remember others' birthdays tend to be 14.1 percent happier.

he spoke about them, "What you are, you are by accident of birth; what I am, I am by myself. There are and will be a thousand princes; there is only one Beethoven."

One's social capital can also be higher inside one group than in another. A woman may have high social capital as a judge in the courtroom, but not be respected in her neighborhood. A man might be respected at church, but not in business. A child may have high social capital on the playground, but not at home.

Building social capital is much like building financial capital. It takes day-to-day habits and routines to develop and maintain relationships. Some of these habits include listening carefully to others' points of view, sending thank-you cards or birthday wishes, lending a helping hand, or just being friendly and waving to our neighbors as we drive by. Over time, one can make investments into their social infrastructure.

As with financial capital, it is often best to diversify and build up social capital in a variety of venues. Those investments must be monitored and managed. In time, they can collectively mature into something of significant value.

Success Circles

When I was young, I figured something out that has turned into a valuable habit. When I wanted to gain a better understanding of a topic, I looked around at the people within my circle of influence and specifically identified role models who had been successful in that area. These are the people I wanted to emulate.

For example, when I was in high school, I went to the person I knew who got the best grades and asked her exactly what her study habits were. When I was choosing a career, I went to the guy I knew who seemed to love his career the most and quizzed him. When I wanted to know about having successful relationships, I sat down with a couple I knew who had a great relationship. When I wanted to make money, I went to the richest

> ### Rich Habit #16
> ### Take Me Out to the Ballgame
>
> Some habits show unexpected correlations and great news for sports fans. Those who regularly attend sporting events have a 45.6 percent better romantic life than those who do not. They also have a whopping 209.5 percent better chance of being "very happy."

guy I knew and I peppered him with a lot of questions. When the people in my success circle speak, I listen intently and take careful notes.

Over time, I had built up this "circle of success" of friends and mentors on whom I could count for the best advice. A lot of this is not really a formal thing—it was just having lunch, playing tennis, or going to a ball game. In every case, I observed that these mentors were always happy to explain their formula for success. I trusted what they said, as they were living examples of the advanced knowledge I needed.

The *We* habits include identifying those in our sphere of influence who have a gift in some specific area, then connecting with them and asking for their insights. This art of connection is one of the most powerful secrets in life. If you are facing a big decision, look around and identify the person you know who is most successful in that area and ask the person exactly how he or she did it.

With my success circle, I specifically targeted people who possessed a gift for the exact issue I was interested in. The other part of this secret is knowing who we should pay less attention to, and there are many. I have often been approached by people wanting me to invest in ventures in which they have no experience. I know someone who has never had a successful relationship in her life, yet she frequently dispenses advice on how to have a successful relationship. I know someone who is a shopaholic who tried to tell me how to save money. I know another person who is overweight who explains how to be physically fit. It is not wise to listen to this kind of advice, it is just noise.

Not all advice is created equal. Some counselors find themselves in positions where they are clearly in over their heads. Some advisors serve to compound the problem. Some therapists are actually using others for their own therapy. Some do considerable damage by over exploration and dismantling personal details. Some who offer counsel are actually just curious and seek personal information for their own amusement. On the flip side, if someone asks for our advice in an area that is outside of our experience, it is best to just say so and, if possible, help this person find the right advisor.

Stick with the winners.[57] Pay attention to those who have actually succeeded and have real-life experience. In many cases, when we need help, the best advice comes from someone within our own circle of influence who has successfully navigated a challenge similar to the one we are facing.

The Stanford Prison Experiment

In an effort to study behaviors in the roles of superiors and subordinates, two groups of students were placed in a mock prison in the basement of a Stanford University building and observed for several days.[58]

Some students were given the role of prisoners, and some were guards. What then occurred has become one of the most fascinating human behavior tests of all time. Students quickly began to manifest either aggressive or rebellious behaviors depending on their role. While everyone knew that this was just a test, the "guards" began to act rigidly and were even hostile toward their "prisoners." They seemed to enjoy the authority and control to a level that clearly went outside acceptable boundaries. In many cases the guards increasingly pushed and even abused their authority, even though their authority was not real.

On the other hand, the prisoners banded together and rebelled against the guards. They planned escapes. They insulted and harassed their captors. At the end of the study, the guards had a very difficult time yielding their authority and resisted releasing their prisoners. The test had to be shut down early and only after outside intervention.

I often joke that if you give someone a badge or walkie-talkie, you will get to see their real character. The illusion of power can be wildly intoxicating. Often those who obtain authority begin to exercise an unfair and even abusive level of control. Toxic leadership is a common phenomenon that can occur in any organization. It is important to take a careful look at an organization's leadership culture.[59]

Authentic leadership is not a position, a calling, or a title. It is not giving great speeches. Authentic leadership is living a life that others will instinctively want to follow; anything less than this is not leadership. It may be position, authority, showmanship, management, dictatorship, or something else, but it is not leadership.

Once I had lunch with Cal Ripken Jr., the great Hall of Fame baseball player who played shortstop for the Baltimore Orioles. He told me about a game wherein he hit a double. As he stood there on second base, he and the shortstop chatted and the shortstop made a comment that it looked like Cal had choked up on the bat a little bit more than usual, and maybe that is why he had hit such a nice double.

Cal told me that he hadn't knowingly choked up on the bat at all, but the comment got into his head and he started to overthink it. It made his head spin a little bit. Then the thought came to him that when he was playing shortstop himself, he might be in a position to make some comments that would make their heads spin too. For a moment, he thought that this might be a good way to get an edge on his competition.

Cal then said that about as soon as this thought occurred, he realized that this was not his style at all. He wanted to preserve the integrity of the game, as well as maintain his own personal integrity. He never went there. Cal is a star, but he did not let it go to his head.

After sitting with Cal Ripken for a couple hours and talking, there was a moment where I thought to myself, "I want to be more like this guy." This was a moment of authentic leadership.

All people who have developed healthy *We* habits will find themselves in situations where they are looked to as an example. There is a variety of leadership styles. Situational leadership is the ability to select the correct style for the appropriate situation.[60] For example, the leadership style of an emergency room doctor who needs to bark orders to quickly save a life needs to be stylistically different from a teacher. However, while styles differ, all great leaders are focused on integrity, elevating the group, and leading by example.

The Real Bikini

In the 1950s, the United States descended on the Marshall Islands and detonated dozens of nuclear bombs. The infamous Bravo test was on the Bikini Atoll, a string of several tiny islands that circle a twenty-four-mile lagoon. Detonated on March 1, 1954, Bravo was the largest atmospheric nuclear explosion in history, with an explosive force equal to nearly one thousand Hiroshima type bombs. It vaporized the test island, parts of two other islands, and left a mile-wide crater in the lagoon floor.

I have done a great deal of work for the Nuclear Claims Tribunal. When I flew over the Bravo Crater site on Bikini, I saw a nearly perfect circular crater in deep blue tropical waters. Littered all around Bikini are similar smaller craters from other blasts—the entire area looks something like a tropical moon. In total, nearly seventy acres of the Bikini Atoll were vaporized by nuclear testing.

The Marshall Islands are a fragile place. I noticed on my first visit that there is a nearly immeasurable distinction between sea and land. There are no hills, mountains, or valleys anywhere. The average elevation is about seven feet above sea level. As we crossed a small bridge in the capital city of Majuro, I was told that it was the highest point in the country, so we named it, "Mount Everest."

Land is scarce; the total land area of the country totals about seventy square miles, which is spread over 375,000 square miles of ocean. The atolls themselves consist of a series of islands and reefs that surround a lagoon. In many areas, there is a small, two-lane road with houses on either side, and the houses themselves front either the lagoon or the ocean. Indeed, in many areas the island is so narrow someone could throw a rock from the ocean side to the lagoon side.

In my entire life, I have never caught anything bigger than an eight-inch trout. But in the Marshall Islands, I felt like the editor-in-chief of Field & Stream. In one quick fishing trip before breakfast, I caught two three-foot tunas and a shark, which I carefully released.

Walking along the beach, I picked up more shells than you could find in all the tourist shops of San Diego, and I found a giant clamshell so large that even two of us couldn't pick it up. I found two more clamshells that weighed in at about fifty pounds each, and I brought one home at the invitation of the island's chief.

As a diver, I had seen plenty of moray eels, but I had never seen such a virgin place where they slept and played right on the shoreline. I followed sea turtle tracks on the sand right up to their nests. I saw schools of thousands of bright tropical fish that cost forty-five dollars each at the pet store at home. The coconut crabs were fascinating. They're the world's largest land crustacean—looking something like a lobster—but they climb coconut trees, cut the coconuts off the branches, and then climb down to eat them by husking the shell with their claws.

The people who inhabit the Marshall Islands, like their environment, are calm and friendly. I had the privilege of accompanying many of the landowners and local people to Rongelap and Rongerik, where much of the nuclear fallout came down. I will never forget my conversations with John, an elderly man who stood on his former home site with me in Rongelap and recalled the day the Bravo nuclear test was conducted.

He had gotten up early to make coffee, and the sun had not yet come up. Suddenly, the sky lit up like it was day. He could see the large mushroom cloud rising off the horizon from Bikini and, soon after, he felt the blast of the shock wave on his face and saw waves breaking in the otherwise calm lagoon.

Later, as the entire village woke up, they watched the radioactive gray ash fall on them, their houses, and their children. John is a calm and kind man. He did not express any anger, only deep sorrow that his one-year-old daughter died from leukemia soon after Bravo.

In declassified documents from the U.S. government, we learn that not only did the military scientists know about the high level of radioactivity on Rongelap, but they were pleased to have the chance to study the long-term effect of radioactivity on humans. In 1994, U.S. Congressman George Miller wrote, "Some Rongelapese have said they believe they were used as guinea pigs to further U.S. understanding of the effects of radiation on humans. In light of recent disclosures regarding actual radiation experimentation in the United States during this period, that possibility cannot be ignored." Congressman Miller also commented on an ongoing thyroid study in the Marshalls. "The findings of the thyroid survey are disturbing. The Committee has been informed that even if only 50 percent of the survey results are verified . . . the [thyroid cancer] incidence rate is still significantly higher, by a factor of 100, than the rate of thyroid cancer found anywhere else in the world."

U.S. Representatives George Miller and Ron de Lugo wrote: "There is no doubt that the AEC (Atomic Energy Commission) intentionally returned (Marshallese) to islands which it considered to be 'by far the most contaminated places in the world,' but which, it told the people, were safe. Nor is there any doubt that the AEC, through the Brookhaven National Laboratory, then planned and conducted test after test on these people to study their bodies' reaction to life in that contaminated environment."[2]

In other words, islanders were purposely resettled on contaminated islands so that the U.S. government could study the long-term effects of radiation on people. It is hard to comprehend. The U.S. government had social roles and responsibilities that not only weren't met, but were blatantly neglected in the Marshall Island operations. Detonating nuclear devices near inhabited islands is wildly stupid. But to knowingly move people back onto contaminated islands is illicit. As a result, billions of dollars were lost, and many innocent lives were harmed or destroyed.

We can learn a lot from this island culture. While traveling to the Marshall Islands and meeting with dozens of the victims who had lost children or become sick themselves, I was surprised that none of them seemed particularly angry. Indeed, they were remarkably calm. In the aftermath of being showered with nuclear fallout and suffering all types of radioactive-related diseases, their attitudes were exactly the opposite of what one might expect. They apparently understood that getting irate would not change the past. They dealt with the problems with dignity and realized, as Winston Churchill said, that "nothing is more costly, nothing is more sterile, than vengeance." They also proved themselves the stronger party, as Mahatma Gandhi once said, "The weak can never forgive. Forgiveness is the attribute of the strong."

Marshall Islands Country Study Guild. Volume 1, Strategic Information and Developments. Published 2013 by International Business Publications, USA, p. 220.

Chapter 9

Influential

Express Yourself

Smile

Human behavioral studies have identified "mirror neutrons" and the human tendency to mimic or react to what we are observing.[61] For example, if we see someone smile, our nervous systems are physiologically pre-programmed to smile back. Or if we see someone who looks angry, we tend to tighten our muscles and stare. Thus, if we want others to be good to us, the most effective means is a *We* habit of spreading kindness ourselves.

In a study called, "The Halo Effect," a lecturer gave the exact same speech to two different groups of students.[62] The content and gestures were identical. In "Speech A" he used a friendly tone. In "Speech B" he used an unfriendly tone. Though actually the same person, the "Speech A" lecturer was consistently given higher scores for his knowledge about his subject.

Being knowledgeable and having good material is not enough. There must be a thoughtful presentation for the message to be accepted. Often, the simple habit of adjusting our tone and smiling can have dramatic

> **Rich Habit #17**
>
> **Spice it Up!**
>
> Putting an effort into romance has benefits. Those who are in satisfying romantic relationships are far more likely to be happy overall and make more money. Those who are in very satisfying romantic relationships are 626.1 percent more likely to be very happy overall. They are also 38.7 percent more likely to earn more than $150,000 per year.

tangible effects. People are naturally attracted to healthy, fun, and positive people.

One day I was having lunch with Denise Brown, a sister of Nicole Brown Simpson, who many believe was murdered by O. J. Simpson. I said something about O. J. that I had heard in the news, and I'll never forget her reply. She said, "Just keep it positive." Just four words, but it made a big impact. I took that to mean, while she had every justification to spend every moment in a rage, she had made a conscious decision to focus on positive things. I respected that. Denise reminded me that, even in adverse times, we can choose our attitude. If we go through life looking in the rearview mirror, we're going to crash.

The *We* habit of a simple smile, an adjustment of tone, or choosing positive attitudes over negative ones, is a remarkably powerful discipline. In socio-economics, the concept is encompassed in the Social Exchange Theory.[63] Just as an accountant calculates "profit equals income minus expenses," so a sociologist states that the value of a relationship is worth its benefits minus its costs.

Benefits can take many forms, such as thoughtful acts, love, humor, listening, kindness, or gratitude. On the other hand, costs can be any number of negative behaviors. By human nature we are all in the habit of sizing up relationships' costs and benefits. If one provides benefits that exceed the costs, then others will want to be with that person and maintain that relationship. If someone has costs that exceed the benefits, one will often end that relationship.

Rich Habit #18
Think "Team Sport"

Healthy people tend to get along with other members of their team and show restraint in what they say. Those who tend to say whatever is on their mind tend to be less educated, as compared to those who are in control of their mouths. Indeed, as restraint goes up, so does the chance of a higher education where doctorate holders are up to 87.8 percent more likely to show restraint.

Social scientists' research shows that the two most important traits for building relationships, families, and marriages are kindness and generosity.[64] With the Social Exchange Theory, an outstanding rule of thumb is to generate at least a six to one ratio of positive benefits to every cost. Said another way, to maintain good relationships we should deliver at least six smiles to every frown.[65] The *We* habits generate a good vibe that elevates others. T. H. Thompson and John Watson said it well, "Be kinder than necessary, for everyone you meet is fighting some kind of battle."

Constructive Criticism

Norman Vincent Peale said, "The trouble with most of us is that we would rather be ruined by praise than saved by criticism."

When I wrote a textbook about measuring the economic effects of disasters titled *Real Estate Damages,* I knew I was pioneering new territory. This was the first book in history on the topic, and I had no beaten path or mentor to follow. When I completed the first draft, I sent it out and invited criticism. And I got it—lots of it! Looking back, the book in its first-draft form would have been a disaster. But by listening to constructive criticism and making several changes, the book was a resounding success.

We need to invite honest feedback, swallow the ego, listen, and act. At the same time, we are not doing anyone a favor when we sugarcoat our criticism and critiques. As Benjamin Franklin said, "Love your enemies, for they tell you your faults."

Put a Cork in It

One common trait among the genuinely smart and powerful is the ability to be silent. As the old saying goes, "We have two ears, but only one mouth."

I was once driving around Chicago with a man who called himself "a little Polish guy" whose father had constantly told him that "you can't learn anything when your mouth is moving, so stick a cork in it!" We had a good laugh about this, but there is a great deal of truth to it. Dale Carnegie said, "You can make more friends in two months by becoming interested in other people than you can in two years by trying to get other people interested in you."

When George Washington presided over the delegation of men who wrote the Declaration of Independence, he could have had a virtual monopoly over the proceedings. Instead, he spoke only once, and that was to basically comment that enough had been done and it was time to wrap it up.[66]

Charles de Gaulle observed that, "silence is the ultimate weapon of power. Remember to never miss a great opportunity to shut up."

Global Cooling

There is a social phenomenon that psychologist Dr. Piero Ferrucci calls "global cooling." Global cooling refers to a trend of fewer small shops and town squares. The impersonal nature of sprawling cities, big-box retailers, busy highways and mega-malls all contribute to this trend of global cooling.

We need *We* habits and virtues that create global warmth, such as courage, patience, and humility. Most important is gratitude, which will bring global warmth most effectively. It was the ancient philosopher Cicero who said, "Gratitude is not only the greatest of virtues; it is the parent of all the others."

Gratitude qualifies as one of the greatest virtues because it offsets global cooling and facilitates kindness, appreciation, and love. With gratitude, we are not only talking about saying a token "thank you" at the grocery store. We are talking about taking a moment to notice another's efforts and hard work and expressing sincere appreciation. Genuine gratitude is a big deal. Studies show that many employees value the feeling of being appreciated as much or more than their paycheck.[68]

> **Rich Habit #19**
> **Get the Word Out**
>
> Positive communication skills add value. Those who tend to be sarcastic tend to be 20.0 percent less happy.

G. B. Stern said, "Silent gratitude isn't much use to anyone." Said another way, unexpressed gratitude is simply ingratitude. People all around us contribute to what we enjoy. With so much abundance, the *We* habits are actually easy to do. We simply take a moment to connect through kindness and genuine appreciation.

There is a lot to be grateful for. In my travels, I am often in places that remind me that three-quarters of the world's population lives on an income of a few dollars a day.[69] If you can read, have enough food to eat, and a nice bed to sleep in, you already enjoy a life of privilege that is not enjoyed by billions of people with whom we share this planet.

Jennifer Merritt, a physics teacher at our local high school, delivered a classic graduation speech that summed up the topic. She suggested that sometimes we trivialize the word "thanks."

> *It has become something we say instinctively, but in our hearts we sometimes overlook the meaning. When someone takes the time to give us a ride somewhere, we say thanks and then get out of the car and go on with our day. But do we truly understand the appreciation that we have just in words given? Being grateful is not something to do, it is something to be.*
>
> *Never forget that there is always something you can be grateful for. Look at this beautiful town you have grown up in, the school you have attended, the friends that you have made, and the family and teachers who have cared for you these last eighteen years. Now think about other people your age around the world and what their lives have entailed these last eighteen years. You have been deeply blessed; remember this.*

There are many ways to express gratitude and create global warming. Put a note of thanks or encouragement on your child's bathroom mirror. Praise your children when they do their chores without being asked. Send a great party photo to the host or a great action photo to your child's coach. Leave a note on the dashboard of your spouse's car that says "thank you" for something nice that he or she did. Put a gift certificate for a back rub given by you in your spouse's pocket. Give your boss a homemade treat. Organize a neighborhood barbeque to honor that elderly neighbor who is always helping everyone out. Look around at those who make your life better and do something that shows you are grateful.

Toxic Extremes

Sometimes we might have the right plan, but the wrong partners. We need to know who to avoid or from whom we should cut close ties.

Sadly, some people's sole role in life seems to be to serve as a bad example. The American Psychological Association defines ten personality disorders and a number of other syndromes and mental diseases.[70] While one may spend a lifetime studying these behaviors, they can be summed up by their extreme positions. The outer extremes of the personality disorders are essentially "hate you" or

> ### Rich Habit #20
> ### Don't Gossip
> Gossip is a buzz kill. Those who never or rarely gossip are 111.1 percent more likely to be happy as compared to those who dish out the dirt.

"love myself" characteristics. The "hate you" extreme is the anti-social personality disorder, often called by the nickname of "sociopath" or in extreme cases, "psychopath." In addition, "borderline personality disorder" characterizes high-conflict people who tend to be bitter and addicted to anger. At the other extreme of the spectrum is the "love myself" narcissist. Among the personality disorders, these three stand out as being especially toxic. Just as *We* virtues compel us to connect with the right people, it is also important that we know who to avoid.

Borderline

As children in elementary school, we used to love playing dodge ball. After splitting into two groups, we would hurl rubber balls at the other team. If we caught a ball being thrown at us, then the person who threw it was out of the game. If we got hit, we were out.

Some balls would miss altogether. Some came at us as soft lobs that were easy to catch. Some came as bullets that hit where it hurt the most. Sometimes several balls would come at us at once. Today, I cannot recall any of the scores, but I can still remember the thrill of the game. Everyone got hit once in a while. I recall seeing some players getting upset, while others just laughed and had fun. Yet some children avoided playing the game altogether.

Life is just one big game of dodge ball. Sometimes it seems as if we get one thing after another thrown at us. I am convinced that in the dodge ball game we call life the score really does not matter. What does matter is if we are enjoying the game.

At times, in the game of life, we all get hit. Happy, healthy people take the hits in stride. They stay in the game of life and have a good attitude.

The easiest way to explain those with "borderline personality disorder" is that these are the people who are playing dodge ball like everyone else, but they are in the habit of being particularly angry and bitter. Borderlines have a difficult time developing and maintaining long-term relationships. They have black belts in complaining. In their embittered state they see the world in strong "black and white" terms of themselves being absolutely right and their "targets," being wrong, a phenomenon that psychologists call "splitting."[71]

Borderlines tend to recruit unsuspecting people to join in their rage, which lasts until their accomplices become targets themselves. They even manufacture drama to feed their addiction to anger. This cycle continues until they ruin all of their relationships and are left alone and bitter.

Sociopaths

Once I took my sons on a shark cage dive. We took a dive boat to Guadalupe Island, located about two hundred miles off the coast of Baja Mexico. With the water chummed with dead fish, we were continuously circled by the largest ocean predator of all, the great white shark.

Great white sharks never live for long in captivity. The only way to see them is in the wild. I felt a little crazy putting on diving gear, getting into a cage, and dropping in the water infested with these huge sharks. When I first saw one, my heart nearly stopped. They are massive. Their mouths could easily bite someone in half. But after watching them circle us for hours on end, I calmed down and started noticing some fascinating predatory behaviors.

First, great white sharks blend in. Their colors match the colors around them and they are remarkably stealthy. I was leaning out of the shark cage getting a video shot of one that was three feet away, when my dive master hit me on the arm, as another shark saw me and was coming straight up for my leg. I pulled back into the cage just in time. I was lulled into a sense of comfort and I almost paid for it in a very big way.

When you miss getting eaten by a great white shark, it creates what we call a "learning moment." Back on the boat, I thought about my research on group behaviors and the "sociopath" predators. Human predators blend in and look and dress like anyone else. Great whites usually swim slowly and make a lot of lazy passes and build a false sense of trust, but all the while their agenda is to eat you. They don't see you as a person; they see you as an object, just as a human predator. Great whites have a knack for spotting easy prey. They have an organ along their side that allows them to monitor their prey's heartbeat, just as human predators seem to have a sixth sense to pick their naive targets.

In a sense great white sharks are cowards, as are human predators. They are not interested in a fair fight. They never take their prey head on. When they do attack, they hit when you're not looking; then they quickly retreat and let their prey bleed to death. Despite what some television shows portray, great white sharks are not just curious. They are not friends or pets. They are the ocean's ultimate ambush killer.

When human predators are caught, they tend to either go into an angry rage or extreme fits of laughter. Either way, their agenda is to do even more harm. Everyone, particularly parents, have a responsibility to watch for the predators.

Contrary to common notions, a sociopath is usually not a bloodthirsty serial killer. In fact, according to Dr. Martha Stout of Harvard University, one out of twenty-four people is an everyday sociopath.[72] Statistically, this means that virtually everyone will come into contact with an everyday sociopath at one point or another. The core problem is that they habitually lie, often when there is no real reason to lie. They do it for a twisted thrill. They have no conscience. In a warped way, they enjoy a feeling of power over people that they deceive. I once knew a sociopath who stole money that was donated to help battered women and felt no remorse whatsoever. Another sociopath faked a nine-month pregnancy for the thrill of the con.

A primary characteristic of a sociopath is superficial charm. With a smile, they can make a pitch to their friends, family, church, schools, and even local Boy Scout troops to raise money for their phony charities or so-called investments. They lie about their credentials and accomplishments. They are dangerous predators and con artists.

During another great white shark dive off the Furlong Islands, I saw about a hundred seals swimming in the shark invested waters. I asked the boat's captain about it, and he told me that when the seals swim together in a group, they are safe. When one of them spots a shark, it alerts the group and they can all out-swim the danger. Great whites do not go after the pack; they go after the vulnerable straggler that wonders off by itself, just as the drug dealer goes after the lonely child or the thief targets the late night straggler on the street. Strong *We* habits create solid relationships to defend against the predators.

The Narcissist

At the other end of the spectrum from the sociopath and the borderline personalities, is the narcissist. While the sociopath takes "hate you" to an extreme, a narcissist takes "love me" way too far.

Narcissists are beyond being selfish, their habits center on self-admiration. They are addicted to attention and will go to staggering lengths to get it. They are remarkably self-centered and talk about themselves endlessly. When there is a conversation and a narcissist walks up, he or she will quickly jump in, hijack the conversation, and turn it to himself or herself. Narcissists think that the world revolves around them and will often show up late to appointments and think nothing of it.

In spite of their perpetual smiles, narcissists are profoundly inconsiderate and oblivious to others. Their guiding light is getting attention and building their personal franchise. They treat everyone else as if he or she has supporting roles in their all-important life. Their life, families, and causes are largely façades, as they actually care very little about anything beyond fueling more attention for themselves and gratifying their own needs.

I once knew a guy who was the poster boy for narcissism. He did all of the above, but there were even more clues. He displayed his medals and trophies by his front door. Nobody got in or out of his house without the opportunity for him to show off his awards. He literally did handstands during dinner events to grab attention. He was remarkably inconsiderate. This narcissist even started giving speeches on ethics, of course using himself as an example. Over time, most people figured him out, just laughed, and shook their heads. He smiled a lot, all while leaving a train wreck of destruction behind him.

Because narcissists are only interested in drawing attention to themselves, they simply suck the energy out of relationships. Like a sociopath, they are toxic and will likely never change. Don't expect an apology, the best resolution is to protect yourself and move on.

Just Get Away

The big three—the sociopath, the narcissist and the borderline—are the predominate personality disorders that one might be most likely to encounter in life.[73] It is less important to make a specific diagnosis, as only a clinical psychologist can do that. What is more important is to be able to identify toxic patterns and behaviors.

The sociopath and narcissist are, in a sense, close cousins. They both tend to have larger-than-life personalities, they both have characteristics that include big smiles and superficial charm, and both will do the unthinkable to achieve their objectives. Neither is likely to be "cured," and they certainly will never seek help or counseling for their conditions. They often attract spouses who hang in there, as long as there's money or some level of prestige or money.

Heaven help their children.

Narcissists and sociopaths often may have a small band of true believers "drinking the Kool-Aid." But they are incapable of engaging in authentic or meaningful relationships. It is damaging to engage with them. They are odd, illogical, and even creepy. One will deliberately deceive and knowingly hurt us, and the other could not care less about us, both are toxic.

The odds are that we will encounter these extreme personalities from time to time. It is important to be sensitive to how people make us feel and have the ability to identify these negative behaviors. Don't waste your time waiting for an apology. It is often futile to confront and it is often best to quietly identify them and then just keep away. The news for borderlines is a little more hopeful. There are therapies and treatments for borderlines, if they have the capacity to recognize their situation and seek help.

Personally, I believe that there is a lot of truth in the old adage that we are the average of the five or six people whom we are closest to. We must be smart enough to surround ourselves with people of high caliber and avoid those who are not. *We* habits involve putting distance between ourselves and toxic people while drawing in good, positive people.

Chapter 10

Cultural

Spice It Up!

The Three-Line Effect

G reat legacies are not created by people who fall into line. They are created by those who have style and a sense of confidence in themselves, those who stand above the crowd.

There is very real pressure to lie down and conform to the norm, and social science has proven it. In an effort to study the effects of peer pressure and conformance, a study was conducted in which a student entered a room where the instructor showed one line, called "Line A," that was next to three other lines of different lengths. While Line A was obviously the same length as Line C, the other students were actually in on the test and by a show of hands intentionally gave wrong answers. The reaction of the new student was observed to see if he or she gave the correct answer or yielded to the crowd.

Most people will follow the crowd, even when the crowd is clearly wrong. Overall, 33 percent of the respondents sometimes conformed to the crowd. Five percent always conformed to the crowd. Remarkably, only 25 percent consistently refused to be swayed by the crowd's blatant, false actions.

Those who enjoy a great legacy did not create it by following the crowd. They did it by being confident in themselves and in their decisions. We have to take a solid stand and speak up when necessary.

Years ago I was flying into Guam on a consulting assignment. As the plane made its approach to land, I noticed a large granite marker in the jungle on the side of a mountain right before the airport. I remembered that Korean Flight 801 had crashed on its final approach into Guam, and realized that that granite monument marked the site of this tragedy. Later, I drove up and found the marker and talked to several people who had been there on the night of the crash. It was a horrible event that still haunts many to this day.

One pilot told me that the approach into Guam is tricky because the terrain comes up so quickly before the airport. In the case of the Korean airliner crash, the co-pilot realized the problem, but was essentially too timid to speak up and tell the pilot.

New rules and regulations were put into place so that the old commander-subservient roles of pilot and co-pilot were replaced by a culture of team effort. Now, for example, pilots call each other by their first name, reducing the feeling of subordination of one above another.

We cannot be timid about important matters. The right thing is not always a compromise. To create a legacy, we must speak up on issues that are important.

McDonalds versus Luby's

In October 1984, a man walked into a McDonald's restaurant in San Ysidro, California, and shot and killed twenty-one people before he was killed by police. It was a horrible tragedy that shocked the nation.

Like all tragedies, there are both emotional and practical issues. A practical problem was what to do with the restaurant building. One night, at about 10:00 p.m., McDonald's bulldozed the building.[75] The next morning, nothing was left but dirt and two palm trees. It was as if McDonald's management somehow thought that by demolishing the building, people would forget what happened.

McDonald's then bought another site just down the street and constructed a new restaurant, which still stands to this day. It is so close to the old site, that some people think it is the location of the original tragedy. In an effort to turn the situation around, McDonald's later donated a million dollars to the victim's families and paid for a memorial. However, in the end, the McDonald's culture was perceived by some as being insensitive.

Sadly, this type of tragedy struck again, but this time it was at Luby's, a chain of cafeteria-styled restaurants. In October of 1991, a man drove his truck through the window of the Killeen, Texas, restaurant. He shot and killed twenty-three innocent people by walking slowly and calmly through the restaurant, talking nicely to some people while shooting others. Eventually, he turned the gun on himself. Now, Luby's has the unfortunate distinction as being the site of the nation's largest mass murder.

Luby's management has always had a habit of treating everyone well. The manager told me, "It may sound corny, but our entire attitude was to treat everyone affected by the tragedy as though they were members of our own family." This attitude was ingrained into the corporate culture and it came through when tragedy struck. Within hours, without any detours to a Madison Avenue public relation firm, company CEO Pete Abeno flew to the site. He immediately offered $100,000 to assist the victims and their families. He went there to help. All the employees were given a paid leave of absence. Psychologists were retained to help with the emotional damage. Through it all, the Luby's sign stayed up.

Impressed by the compassion and kindness of corporate leadership, the city of Killeen petitioned Luby's to not abandon the site but, rather, to reopen the facility. The management conceded and extensively remodeled the property and reopened the restaurant about five months later. It went on to enjoy business as usual.

Luby's had a culture of *We* habits such as openness, kindness, consideration, and treating others well. Luby's was a victim like everyone else; they lost employees in the tragedy. However, they faced the problems head on. They faced the cameras and they took the high road throughout it all.

The Trophy Generation

Every person can be a champion in something. Everyone has a gift. However, a football player's gift is not to be a jockey—he or she might kill the horse! Celebrities' gifts are not to be politicians, although some try. The point is that everyone has a gift in something, but nobody has a gift in everything. Everyone can be a winner at some things, but a loser in others.

The "trophy generation" describes children who were raised in an "everyone's a winner" culture of continual and unearned admiration. Their shelves and closets are filled with trophies for games they actually lost, certificates where there were no actual achievements, and outlandish medals for simply showing up. These awards have no authentic meaning. We are producing a generation of delusional, entitled children who have a warped sense of privilege.

The trophy generation has been damaged by well-intended, yet detrimental actions of parents, teachers, and others who wanted to protect these children from the harsh realities of the world. These children often have considerable trouble adjusting to life as it really is. Just as a muscle must have resistance to develop, our *We* habits must include exercises that actually challenge ourselves and allow us to take our losses in stride.

Every child has fears and gets a little emotionally beat up once in awhile. My own son came home and complained that he didn't have any friends, but I knew that wasn't true and I didn't buy into it. I told him, "Toughen up buttercup!"

A couple of months later, he ran for class president and won. Children test us and try to get us to take on all their battles, but we can't protect them from all the realities of life. We need to let them get out there, work through their struggles, and grow.

Conflict Resolution

Sometimes when a group gets together—a family goes on vacation or people get together for a camp out—there is a predictable cycle. Introduced by Bruce Tuckman in 1965, the Tuckman Stages of Group Development are to *form, storm, norm, and perform*.[76] "Form" is where the group comes together, "storm" is the inevitable group conflict, "norm" is when the dust settles, and "perform" is when everyone pulls together as a team toward their objectives.

Strong *We* habits include those skills for dealing with the storm so that we can move forward to norm and perform.

There are many ways to successfully work through conflict. Perhaps the first rule of conflict resolution is to control the impulse to jump in and instead just listen. Reflective listening is where one carefully listens and simply repeats back what was heard. This is done to both clarify our understanding and assure the other party that he or she is indeed being heard. Simply listening can resolve many conflicts.[77]

With many smaller issues, we can realize that we do not have to attend every argument we are invited to. We can pick our battles and just walk away. If we want others to put up with our issues, we need to cut them some slack. One man who is legendary in my community was famous for saying, "If you can allow people three idiosyncrasies, then you can get along with just about anyone."

> ### Rich Habit #21
> ### Cut the Potty Mouth
> Profanity correlates wit h a lack of education, with doctorates having a 60.8% lower chance of having a potty mouth compared to those with a high school education.

Often we must choose between winning an argument or winning a friend, and letting go may be the best solution.

It is important that we consciously make decisions about the people we associate with. As George Washington said, "Associate yourself with men of good quality if you esteem your own reputation, for 'tis better to be alone than in bad company."

We all need some boundaries as to what we will and will not accept. If we do need to get involved, we can always follow the adage to "say what you mean without being mean." It is one thing to be brutally honest, and another to be constructively honest. No matter what, another's bad behavior is not justification for any type of bad behavior on our part, as we have a responsibility to keep our side of the street clean.

Ultimately, conflict resolution essentially comes down to four options; aggressive, assumptive, agreeable, and assertive. Being aggressive can come off as pushy, angry, and defensive. Right or wrong, the aggressive person might get results but lose respect. Attorneys who are losing their case will often just yell louder.

On the other hand, if the accusation is false, remaining silent and being assumptive means that we do not defend ourselves, perhaps by believing that we are taking the high road. Yet, by remaining silent, there can be an assumption of guilt, or what the legal community calls an "implied admission." Furthermore, assumptive behavior can result in being a pushover or taken for granted.

> ### Rich Habit #22
> ### Catch the Wave
>
> Those who wave to their neighbors are up to 69.8 percent more likely to be very happy compared to those who do not. Furthermore, of those who have more than $1 million in net assets are 63.8 percent more likely to wave to their neighbors, as compared to those who are in debt.

For example, if a co-worker makes a comment that implies you are lazy, and you don't speak up, your silence might be assumed to mean you are guilty.

The two more healthy approaches are being agreeable or assertive. If the accusation is true, we are better off by taking responsibility. By being agreeable, we admit faults and make amends. Some time ago, my daughter was giving my youngest son a hard time. This went on for a couple of weeks. One day, I taped a note to her bathroom mirror that said, "Your true character is revealed by how you treat your little brother." I was proud of the fact that she got the message, took responsibility, and changed her behavior. Today, they adore each other.

Being assertive means that we stand up for ourselves, but we do it with dignity. When dealing with a difficult person, the BIFF rule often applies—be *brief, informative, firm, and friendly.*[78] We keep our communications short and to the point, stating just the facts and avoiding being either pushy or a pushover.

Ultimately, if there is a real problem, then generally the best approach is to be assertive and stand up for ourselves, while keeping petty emotions in check. The best people I know who have mastered conflict resolution can say everything with a smile. They know that smiles are contagious and they can steer conversations in a positive way.

With any conflict, we should be aware of all the options and have the insight to select the best approach. In the end, we can love others for what they are and forgive them for what they are not. Abraham Lincoln also had some great advice when he said, "The best way to destroy your enemies is to turn them into your friends."

Forgiveness

As I work on disasters around the world, I am frequently with people who have been wronged. I have spent time with the victims of crimes, environmental spills, faulty construction, terrorist attacks, nuclear testing, and more. For many years, I have made a number of observations.

Forgiveness is the ability to completely let go of anger and resentment toward another person or organization. In practical terms, it is always easier to forgive someone who apologizes and, where applicable, pay restitution. Certainly, if someone has done something wrong, sincerely apologizes, and does whatever he or she can to correct the situation, we have a duty to accept the apology and not harbor resentment. Likewise, when we have done something wrong, we cannot move forward without first apologizing and doing whatever is necessary to correct our course and never go back to this behavior again.

However, sometimes we are faced with situations where there has been an offence or crime, and the offender lacks the character and ethics to apologize. The person may be an everyday sociopath who simply goes through life without a conscience and who is past feeling. The situation may be improved somewhat if the perpetrator is caught, reprimanded, demoted, fired, or imprisoned. However, even for the worst offences, a perpetrator may never get caught or apologize, and justice may never be served. These are the hardest situations for forgiveness.

While it is difficult, it still must be done. One cannot have a healthy life or build new relationships without getting past the upsets of the past. Not forgiving keeps us in the struggle. We must move effectively through the "Five Stages of Grief"—*Denial, Anger, Bargaining, Depression,* and *Acceptance.* Only upon the final stage of acceptance can we move forward.

To forgive, the first step is to dismiss some notions, such as "forgive and forget." While that makes sense with lots of life's daily bumps and bruises, no reasonable person could forget a murder, abusive behavior, or other serious situation. While time can play a major role in dulling the pain, there are simply some conditions that cannot successfully be forgotten. In fact, some psychologists say that premature forgiveness damages the subconscious mind and that one cannot forgive until he or she has fully felt the pain that has been caused.

Forgiveness does not mean acceptance of bad behavior or the offender. Indeed, the greatest misconception about forgiveness is that we are required to somehow reconcile with the perpetrator. Forgiveness should not be confused with reconciliation. No rational, kind, and forgiving person could ever accept or condone the atrocities of the Holocaust, September 11, child abuse, or other horrible events. We may very well need to distance ourselves from someone who has ongoing toxic behavior, and in some cases, we have every right and responsibility to do so. Forgiveness does not mean having to waive our legal rights.

To forgive, we must first dispel the myths. Forgiveness does not require forgetting, acceptance of bad behavior, or reconciliation. The word "forgiveness" is built on the root word "give." The key of forgiveness is that it is a choice we make to benefit ourselves, not so much the offender. Indeed, no one benefits from forgiveness more than the one who forgives. While you may give the offender the release of your hatred or fury, more importantly you give yourself the ability to let go of negative feelings and move on.

Anger and resentment are like a ball and chain locked onto our ankle, keeping us from where we want to go. To not forgive means remaining angry, resentful, bitter, vindictive, and miserable. To forgive, we could ask ourselves some questions: "Do I let go and move ahead with my life or do I spend my time stuck where I am and consumed by somebody else's bad behavior?" "Does my desire to do something positive for myself and those I love outweigh my hatred and anger?" "Are my time, energy, and emotional health worth wasting on this situation?" One political leader, pointing at chronic wars between two groups, stated that the conflicts could only end when both parties decided to love their own children more than they hate each other.

Forgiveness is an internal outlook on people, situations, and life. Robert Enright, a developmental psychologist at the University of Wisconsin, explains, "Forgiveness is giving up the resentment to which you are entitled and offering to the person who hurt you friendlier attitudes to which they are not entitled." People who forgive are at peace with themselves. They let the small stuff go altogether. They are not easily offended.

For some situations, forgiveness may take considerable time, and it may come in steps, but once we make that choice to forgive, we can let go of a host of negative conditions and direct our attention to healing and being positive and productive. Reverend Karyl Huntley said, "You know you have forgiven someone when he or she has harmless passage through your mind."

Science has even recognized the benefits of forgiveness, which have been linked to alleviating chronic pain, easing depression, and reducing stress levels.[79] Forgiveness is one of the key coping mechanisms that even helps those who are ill to heal quicker. In all its forms, letting go allows us to move forward.

Leniency

When my youngest son was four years old, he had a knack for diffusing perilous situations with his charm. Once he was misbehaving, and we said, "When are you going to behave?" to which he replied, "Not yet!" We laughed so hard that he once again "walked" for his crimes.

As seniors in high school, my friends and I spent a considerable amount of time thinking of what we could do to amuse ourselves by way of various pranks. Our supreme accomplishment was what we called "fire-extinguishing." This exercise would start by first getting a fire extinguisher, filling it with water, and then using the tire hose at the gas station to pressurize it. Then, we'd drive around squirting people. At the time, the movie *Jaws* was drawing large lines at the local theater. Our goal was to squirt every person in the entire line. We learned that one fire extinguisher would not do the trick, so we acquired several more and returned to the next showing where we accomplished our goal. We were greatly amused by our success.

Hungry from our activities, we headed for dinner at the drive through and squirted the guy at the window. Swaggering with that success, we then got the brilliant idea to put a fire extinguisher up one of our guys' jackets with the hose down his arm. He walked into the restaurant and squirted all the patrons.

The next day at school, an announcement came over the loud speaker asking that a short list of boys go to the principal's office. Oddly, that list of individuals matched exactly with everyone in our car the night before.

While I joked with my friends as we walked down the hall, I was scared. I went trembling to the principal's office where I had the opportunity to meet with Detective Johnson of the Fullerton Police Department. I had heard that confession was good for the soul, so I quickly admitted my part of the crime. He asked for my dad's work phone number. I immediately wondered what was supposed to be so good about confession. He then told me that he would give me a day to tell my dad myself before he called him. He knew that I was going to have a bad night.

When I went home, I was terrified. I sat in my room with a big pit in my stomach. I was shaking. I finally told my older brother my dilemma, and he told me to just get it over with. I walked into the kitchen and said, "Dad, I gotta tell you something," and then I spilled the beans. Expecting to be grounded for life, I'll never forget his reply: "Son, I'm very mad. It sounds like you had a lot of fun, and I'm upset that you didn't invite me to go with you!" Then he laughed and laughed.

By simply watching me slink into the kitchen and by listening carefully as I poured out my tale, my dad knew that I had already been through enough. My dad could have pounded me with a harsh punishment, but he could see that I would never be so stupid again. Instinctively, he knew that under-regulation results in chaos and over-regulation results in resentment. The challenge we all face is to find a balance.

Style and Integrity

Once I was on a business trip in New York. As I often do, I had one of my children with me, and this time it was my oldest son. When we got into a taxi, my son found a high-end smartphone. We were trying to figure out who it belonged to when the phone rang. I answered it and on the other end was a frantic man looking for his lost phone. I told him to meet my son outside of the New York convention center. A few minutes later, my son came in and told me that the man had come to get his phone, and that he was so happy that he offered my son a hundred dollars. He loves money, but he turned down the cash. He knew that he was simply returning something to the rightful owner, and I was proud of that decision.

On another occasion, I was walking through a parking lot in Los Angeles with one of my business partners, Orell Anderson. All of a sudden, he stopped, took a quarter out of his pocket, and put it into a parking meter. I asked him why he had done this. He noticed that a meter maid was coming down the street and that someone had parked his or her car and the meter was expired; he didn't want the person to get a ticket. He had no idea who owned the car, but he thought that he would help the person out anyway.

I was impressed with his level of kindness toward a person he would never meet. But this is the kind of guy he is. He doesn't need any thanks or praise for it, he just likes to help others.

Albert Schweitzer said, "Do something for somebody every day for which you do not get paid." With the *We* habits, challenge yourself to do those little things that can be a big deal for someone else.

Good Manners

When I directed a group in a large consulting firm, I hired some of the brightest minds in the field. Their poor table manners with clients, however, were a serious problem. One guy would sit and lick his spoon like a lollipop. Then he would eat using his fork like a lever as he rotated his plate around. I asked him why he did this and he told me, true to his engineering background, that it was a more efficient form of eating.

Two guys would smear their entire piece of bread with butter and prop it up in their hand throughout the entire lunch so they could take a bite anytime. Still another would eat pseudo-European style, so that he would not have to trade hands with his utensils and thus could plow through his lunch more quickly. Elbows on the table were standard. When it came to a technical problem, they were the best, but when it came to good manners it was almost comical, except the clients weren't laughing.

One client confided in me that he passed over using one of my guys because he was concerned, not with his professional qualifications or intelligence but that his manners might come off poorly in front of others. Now the situation had gone from being an annoyance to costing business. It was my little in-house etiquette disaster, and I had to do something.

After thinking about it, I decided to have a "boot camp" day where we would discuss a variety of administrative and technical issues. During lunch, I hired a "Miss Manners" to address the group on the topic of business and dining etiquette. I had a long conversation with her, telling her about the behavior that was causing the embarrassment.

The session went pretty well, but when Miss Manners wasn't looking, one of the guys would make faces. Not surprisingly, he was the worst offender. After being instructed on the fundamentals of dining etiquette, we all ate lunch while Miss Manners watched us and took notes. Most of the group got the message and did well, but of course there were slip-ups. Her name was Diana, so we decided that if any of us were violating any of the rules of manners in front of a client, we could tip off our colleague by saying, "Oh by the way, Diana called." If the offense was really out of bounds, we would say, "Diana called, and she said it was an emergency!"

It was not a matter of acting superior. Good etiquette is simply showing others that you respect them enough to behave appropriately.

Parenting

On one of my frequent business trips, I was reading a book about my roles and responsibilities in raising my children. As I was reading, I became increasingly concerned that there was no way I'd remember all the information. I realized, though, that there was one simple theme to the book—spend time with my children. In fact, the whole book could be summed up with the old adage, "Children spell love: t-i-m-e."

I have always felt that my basic duties demanded that I support my family, but I wanted to do more than just my basic duties. The Dalai Lama says, "A loving atmosphere in your home is the foundation for your life."

At that point, I decided to do two things: First, I committed to frequently take one of my children out to lunch or dinner. This would give us a chance for old-fashioned one-on-one time. I thought this would be a good thing, but I had no idea just how great an idea this was. When I got to the elementary school to pick my children up, they were just bursting at the seams to see me. They would tell all of their friends that they were going out to lunch with their dad. The whole class would stare as I picked them up. I got to meet a lot of their friends, so I had faces to put with the names I heard about at dinner every night.

At times they tell me everything, and we talk about things that I think many children would not discuss with their parents. Other times, we don't talk about much. There is no agenda, except to hang out together. They know that I sincerely love them, not just by my telling them, but by taking a little time to step out of my expected role.

Next, I decided to take one of my children at a time on business trips whenever possible. I realized that I can fly one of my children and me in coach for the price of one first-class ticket. On my first accompanied business trip, I took my oldest son to New Mexico where I was doing research at the National Atomic Museum.

On my next business trip, I took my seven-year-old son to San Antonio. After a day on the plane, in rental cars, and getting lost, we finally sat down at a restaurant near our hotel. To me, it was just another business trip. When we got to the restaurant, I asked my son what the best day in his life had been. I expected him to tell me about a particularly profitable Christmas or birthday, but I nearly fell off my seat when he told me that it was that day—today. While it was just another trip for me, for this little guy it had been an incredible adventure to go on a business trip with his dad.

Realizing that this was so important to my son, I changed my attitude and focused on ensuring that this would be a great trip for him. We went to the hotel and got every pamphlet about every available tour and place of interest. We took a ghost-hunting tour, visited the Alamo, took a river boat ride, went to Ripley's Believe It or Not—which featured real shrunken heads that my son still talks about—we saw two I-Max movies, and ate lots of Texan food.

My first such trip with my daughter was to San Francisco. She was just four years old. She almost came out of her skin with excitement about her trip. My daughter had her Barbie backpack with all kinds of treats and a little camera. People stopped to watch my little girl in the airport with her Barbie roll-along suitcase. After my meetings, we walked around Fisherman's Wharf, played in the sand, and ate ice cream. She still talks about going down the "crooked road"—Lombard Street. When she got older, I took her on a business trip to the Bahamas. As I worked, she took scuba lessons. About fifteen minutes after my daughter became certified, I joke that I took advantage of that country's more lenient child-endangerment laws and took her on a shark dive.

Once I agreed to give a speech in Florida, so I took my son out of school; he came to the conference and then spent two days surfing. Another time my daughter and I chartered a plane and flew over the mysterious Nazca Lines in Peru. Since these trips, there have been many others. We treasure all of the trips and great times we have had on these business trips throughout the years.

Chapter 11

The Next Step for *We*

Snicker Doodles

E very once in a while, my family gets out the baking pans and makes one of my favorite things, snicker doodle cookies. One day, we were making cookies and I reviewed the list of ingredients that included flour, baking powder, water, eggs, cinnamon, butter, sugar, and cream of tartar. I noticed that none of the individual ingredients sounded very good by itself. In fact, on their own, some of them could make one gag. But blended together, they culminate into a pinnacle life experience, at least for me.

No great achievement was ever accomplished alone. It takes a diverse group that blends and works well together. Creating synergy with the right people is essential to great pursuits. Einstein would frequently take long walks on the Princeton campus with a small group of close associates. On those walks, he would engage in deep conversations about politics, religion, physics, and his unified field theory.

History's spiritual, philosophical, and religious figures all clearly applied strong *We* habits of charity, kindness, and love. After preparing

> **Rich Habit #23**
>
> **Enjoy Dinner as a Family**
>
> Those who have sit-down dinners with their families are 40.7 percent more likely to be happy, over those who do not and 60.8 percent more likely to be satisfied with their romantic life. They are also 43.6 percent more likely to earn over $100,000 annually.

for His ministry by going into solitude for forty days and forty nights, Jesus then connected with twelve disciples. He primarily taught us to love God and love our neighbors as ourselves—the pinnacle *We* habit.

Buddha taught that happiness never decreased by being shared. He observed that thousands of candles can be lit from a single candle, and the life of the candle will not be any worse for it. Muhammad taught his followers, "You will not enter paradise until you have faith. And you will not complete your faith until you love one another."

Socrates stated, "Be slow to fall into friendship; but when thou art in, continue firm and constant." Plato observed, "Any man may easily do harm, but not every man can do good to another." Aristotle said that, "no one would choose a friendless existence on condition of having all the other things in the world."

Connecting with Others

I'm often reminded of the old story where a grandfather and grandson are walking along the beach. As they walked, the grandfather would pause every time he saw a sand dollar, pick it up, and throw it into the sea. His grandson asked why he did this, and the grandfather replied that if the sand dollar were not in the water, it would dry out and die. The young boy said that this did not seem so smart to him because with so many sand dollars, it would be impossible to make any real difference. The grandfather picked up another sand dollar, threw it into the sea, and then said, "Well, it will make all the difference in the world to that one."

Being there for others is important. Connection with family and close friends is crucial. There is a story of a

Rich Habit #24
Family First

When listing top accomplishments, children clearly ranked number one and far outranked college, career, or health.

Greatest Accomplishment

Category	Index
Children	503
Family	183
College	174
Career	118
Marriage	112
Friends	59
General relationships	59
Health	35
Finding happiness	31
Teaching	31

grandfather who gathered his family around his death bed. He picked the youngest grandchild and gave her a pencil. He asked her to break it, and she easily did. The grandfather then took a handful of pencils and handed them to his tall, strong grandson. He told him, holding them all together, to try and break them in half. The grandson tried and tried, but couldn't.

Like any family, this family had its struggles. There were the unfortunate remarks, the disputes, the zany aunt, the wild cousin, and the idiot uncle. But on the whole, the family would fare better sticking together than becoming estranged. The dying grandfather then told his family that it was his single wish that the family would always recognize the strength and the value created by staying close.

The Gratitude Box

Near my desk sits a remarkable box. I got it at an outdoor fair on a trip I took to Australia with my oldest son. The colors and textures of the wood are stunning. In all my years, I have never seen anything like it. This box was handmade by a man who crafts his boxes by hand using exotic woods that only grow "down under." It is a prized possession itself, and I use it to hold something that is of remarkable value.

Inside my gratitude box is a pen, some wax, a box of matches, a roll of postage stamps, and a sterling silver signet ring with an impression of our family's crest. Also inside are some simple thank-you cards. Whenever someone does something that enriches my life, which is often, I write his or her name on a piece of paper and put it into my gratitude box.

Once a week I have a quiet ritual. I take my gratitude box, open it, and read each name. I then write a thank-you note to each person. Once I write the note, I put it in an envelope and strike a match to make a wax seal with the ring. I love the smells of the sulfur in the matches and melting wax. The whole process is a rare relief from telephones, computers, and technology.

My ritual is pure old school. I know that it would be quicker and easier to shoot an e-mail or text, but that does not do it for me. As I write each card, I focus on that person and my gratitude for him or her. I also think about what I can do to emulate the person's kindness and pay it forward. The gratitude box ritual is my cornerstone *We* habit.

The *We* Challenge Coin

This is where you accept the challenge coin and take responsibility for your own *We* cornerstone. This is where you do something to build relationships; specifically, stay connected, elevate your group, express yourself, and spice it up!

Avoid the January 4th effect. Pick only one new *We* habit and make it simple. For example, don't commit to sending ten thank you cards a month; rather, commit to sending one, but more if you choose to.

Commit to mastering your new *We* habit and make it a solid cornerstone of your life. Here are some suggestions, or come up with one of your own:

Sit down to a family dinner _____times per week.

Call a family member or friend _____times per week to say hello.

Have lunch or coffee with a friend _____times per week.

Do a fun activity with your spouse or partner every _____.

Spend at least _____hours playing with your children every day.

Listen to others completely before you speak.

Resolve all arguments before you go to bed.

Forgive_____and let it go.

Send a thank-you card to someone _____times per month.

Remember birthdays by sending cards or making birthday phone calls.

Smile every time you make eye contact with someone.

Give up swearing.

Make a list of your core success circle.

Identify toxic behaviors and get away from_____.

Wave at the neighbors.

Expand your social circle.

Say thank you to the retail clerks and anyone who helps you.

Define your own style of_____.

SECTION 3
THE *DO* CORNERSTONE

We do the things we need to do,
so we can do the things we want to do

Chapter 12
The *Do* Habits

Three Factors of Productivity

The first cornerstone, *Me,* is a point of beginning and our level of mental illumination. The second cornerstone, *We,* is where we connect with others. The third cornerstone has Do habits that generate utility and productivity. It is also known as the *Servium* cornerstone, which is the Latin declaration, *I will serve.* The *Do* habits affirm our productivity. Here, we do the things we have to do, so that we can do the things we want to do.

The world belongs to the productive. The elements of economic theory states that productivity results from combining land, labor, and capital. In other words, to be productive we are conscientious with our land, with home or work space, our labor or physical health, and our financial capital.

The *Do* habits involve doing our chores, taking care of our health, and earning a living. We commit to doing our to-do lists and our jobs with a

> **The *Do* Cornerstone**
>
> The third cornerstone Do is productivity. From it comes our "to do" lists for physical fitness, financial fitness and maintaining our home and work space.

quality mind-set. Dr. Martin Luther King, Jr., said, "If a man is called to be a street sweeper, he should sweep the streets even as Michelangelo painted or as Beethoven composed music or as Shakespeare wrote poetry. He should sweep streets so well that all the hosts of heaven and earth will pause to say, here lives a great street sweeper who did his job well."

Heaven's Gate

While a positive mind-set elevates ourselves and those around us, the opposite is also true. The negative side of one's daily habits can be illustrated with a case involving the United States' greatest mass suicide.

The Heaven's Gate mansion was located near San Diego in Rancho Santa Fe. The property sat on three acres, and the nine-thousand-square-foot home had nearly every imaginable amenity including a swimming pool, spa, sauna, and even an elevator. The cult members rented the house; the lease specifically limited occupancy to just seven people, yet they added many more.

On March 26, 1997, police discovered the bodies of thirty-nine members of the Heaven's Gate cult. Bodies were found in nearly every room of the seven bedroom house. The bodies were all located on beds or bunk beds, with identical purple shrouds over their heads and duffel bags by their sides. For reasons nobody knows, the cult members all had quarters in their pockets, and wore black trousers and black Nike shoes. The group left a "farewell video" in which they explained that they believed they were discarding their bodies or "earthly vehicles" to return to a spaceship that followed the Hale-Bopp comet.

> ### Rich Habit #25
> ### Make Your Bed
>
> Those who do their chores and keep their living space more tidy, tend to make more money. For example, those who make their bed in the morning are up to 206.8 percent more likely to be millionaires, as compared to those who have a negative net worth.

This was one of the strangest events in world history. The property owner contacted me just as the coroner's office was finishing the task of removing all the bodies. My first trip to the house was sickening. After spending my first day there, my suit smelled so bad that when I arrived back home, I jumped in the pool with my suit still on.

I visited the house on dozens of occasions, and each time I noticed something else more bizarre. For starters, *everything* inside the house had been labeled. Every light switch, electrical outlet, shelf, cupboard, jar, and container had a small label stating exactly what it turned on or what was contained inside. This labeling extended right down to which light switch illuminated the kitchen sink. Initially, this habit of labeling confounded me until one day when I was walking through the house with a colleague. She suggested that the cult's leader, Doe, wanted to create an environment where all the thinking was already done regarding what to wear, what to eat, and how the money was spent.

Everything was done Doe's way. At the same time, no cult member was allowed to be alone. Monitoring devices were everywhere. There was a bizarre amount of wiring throughout the house and even down the chimney to listen in on every conversation. Even when cult members spoke on the phone, someone was always there to listen in and monitor them. A cult member could not visit the bathroom by themselves. This extreme environment virtually eliminated the need for a person to think independently about even the slightest detail.

While the press never knew it, the cult had sent a suicide letter to the home's owner. The tone of the letter suggested that they were actually doing the owner a favor by creating a famous event that would make the house an invaluable shrine. This was clearly yet another one of their delusions. In reality, the cult did the owner no favors at all. After the house was cleared of the bodies and their belongings, significant physical damage remained, which amounted to well over $200,000. Looking for some kind of break, my client tried to appeal his property taxes, only to receive a letter in return from the San Diego Assessor's Office that rejected his appeal on the grounds that a mass suicide in his property did not qualify as a tragedy. Eventually, he was forced to give the property back to the bank. The bank, in turn, sold it at a deep discount to a nearby neighbor who promptly had the house bulldozed.

At every disaster site that I study, I look for the lessons. Here it was clear that our environment and daily routines have a profound effect on behavior. What surrounds us becomes part of us. If left in the wrong environment long enough, even the most sensible person can succumb to veering off course.

Doe used the force of simple daily habits to brainwash his followers into some insane notions. I spent many days in that house studying every aspect of life within the Heaven's Gate mansion. There was nothing dramatic about most of the habits and rituals he implemented. Doe took it a step at a time. He created a closed environment. He instituted daily routines that spread out gradually, more and more toward the bizarre. Over time, the daily routines added up until Doe had total and complete control.

Ultimately, when the cult's leader announced that the males should get castrated and that they should all "shed their vehicles" to join a spacecraft, their ability for independent and objective thinking had been successfully eliminated. Consequently, thirty-eight other people lost their ability to reason and committed mass suicide.

Daily habits are a remarkable power that add up to who we are. As Heaven's Gate shows, bad habits pile up and create a negative force that pulls people down. On the other hand, good habits also pile up and are a powerful force to build people up. We make those tiny but critical decisions every day. Our daily *Do* habits, good or bad, all add up and ultimately determine our level of productivity and ultimately our destiny.

Keep in Shape

Pump It Up!

Originally stated by the German scientist Rudolf Clausius, the Second Law of Thermodynamics states that anything in the physical world that is not acted upon will eventually result in chaos or decay.

In other words, our physical health will go to shambles if we don't continuously intervene and act. In a business context, the same is true for our products and services.

This is a critical scientific observation. Everything else becomes compromised or even irrelevant if one's physical condition is shot. Good health care is essential. If we are not actively maintaining and improving our health, then the forces of nature will tear it down. This is the law of physics. Acceptance of this principle is crucial to being healthy.

> **Rich Habit #26**
> **Get Some Sleep**
>
> Getting enough sleep strongly correlates to wealth, happiness, romance, and education. Those who do are 25.2 percent more likely to have a college degree.

The Pareto Principle

The Pareto Principle sets forth the well-known 80:20 ratio that represents how a minority can have the majority of effect. For example, some believe that 80 percent of success is enjoyed by 20 percent of the people, 20 percent of salesmen get 80 percent of the sales, or 20 percent of the people cause 80 percent of the change. Some believe that 20 percent of the people do 80 percent of the work. This principle can apply to a number of things, including the *Do* habits of taking care of our health.

To be most productive, we must maintain the standard routines of eating right, exercising, and taking care of our basic hygiene, at least most of the time.

It may be okay to take a break and lay around like a slob on vacation or on a weekend once in a while, but for the most part, we need to stay on top of these things.

Eating right is a key *Do* habit. This is particularly true today when our bodies are inherently designed to store fat in times of plenty to prepare for a famine, but the famine never comes.[80] So, many just tend to store more and more fat. Much of the food industry has largely moved away from fresh foods to processed sugars and flour that lack nutrition but stimulate the pleasure zones of the brain to crave more and more. Fast food, like all industrial convenience food, is professionally designed to maximize reward value and is therefore often exceptionally fattening and unhealthy.[81]

As a society, we are experiencing an epidemic characterized by increasing rates of obesity, hypertension, the metabolic syndrome, type two diabetes, and kidney disease.[82] From 1971 to 2000, the prevalence of obesity in the United States increased from 14.5 percent to 30.9 percent. Unhealthy diets and sedentary behaviors have been identified as the primary causes of deaths attributable to obesity.[83] While fad diets have us cutting out fats or focusing on high

---

Rich Habit #27

Add Value

Of all habits, a "strong work ethic" ranked #1 as the habit people were most proud of. This was true across the board for low and high earners alike.

All Time Best Habits

Strong work ethic	370
Loyalty family/friends	327
Care about others	263
Eat healthy	207
On time	150
Organized	141
Honest	125
Exercise	114
Reading	87
Attend church	28

protein, it comes down to "calories in and calories out." Research shows that in order to gain weight, more calories need to enter your body than are being burned. If more calories leave your body than enter it, then you lose weight.[84] Personally, I don't care what the diet-of-the-month says, it is not much more complicated than that.

Processed foods pack large amounts of calories into packages that make us crave more. The processed foods are the main reason why people all over the world are getting fat and sick.[85] These foods often include massive amounts of processed sugars. One pizza shop owner once quietly admitted to me that he started selling more pizzas when he spiked the dough with table sugar. These massive amounts of added sugars are detrimental to one's health.[86]

A major culprit of sugar are soft drinks and juices. Sugar has addictive properties similar to drugs like cocaine.[87] Sugar-sweetened beverages like soft drinks and fruit punches contain large amounts of readily absorbable sugars that contribute to weight gain and an increased risk of type two diabetes.[88] Consumption of sugar-sweetened beverages, particularly carbonated soft drinks, may be a key contributor to the epidemic of overweight and obesity, by virtue of these beverages' high added sugar content, low satiety, and incomplete compensation for total energy.[89] This added sugar contains no essential nutrients, is bad for our teeth, is high in fructose, which can overload the liver, and can cause insulin resistance.[90] The fruit juice at the supermarket may not be what you think it is, even if it's labeled as "100 percent pure" and "not from concentrate." After being squeezed from the fruit, the juice is often stored in oxygen-depleted holding tanks for up to a year before it is packaged.[91]

> **Rich Habit #28**
> **Get the Lead Out**
>
> Taking care of one's health ranked as the number one *Do* habit that people were most proud of. Of those who have good health, "exercise" was ranked as the number one best habit, while exercise is not even among the top ten habits of those in poor health. To sum it up, if you exercise, you are far more likely to earn more money, have a higher net worth, be better educated, and have better romance. Plus, those who exercise are 23.2 percent likely to be happy overall.

Society has been told that saturated fat is unhealthy. It is claimed to raise cholesterol levels and give us heart attacks. However, other studies suggest that the true picture is more complicated than that.[92] These studies suggest that neither saturated fat nor dietary cholesterol cause harm in humans. Research shows that the low-fat dogma was based on flawed studies that have since been debunked.[93] Furthermore, long-term studies show that low-fat diets generally do not reduce the risk of heart disease, cancer or other major lifestyle diseases.[94]

The "Full Glass Theory" - where good habits are just poured in until the bad habits are crowded out and disappear—applies to many areas, including our health. Once we "go on a diet" we are doomed.[95] Restricting something makes it craved all the more. Instead, we can drink so much water and eat so many fresh vegetables and fruits, that there simply is little or no room for the junk.[96] We can lose weight by visiting with our doctors, reducing calories, limiting sugars and starches, eating lean protein, fat, and vegetables, and by exercising three or four times a week.[97] This simple strategy helps keep us healthy and productive.[98] Of course, much of nutrition comes down to common sense and basics, but new nutritional information is continually coming out, so it is a good idea to keep abreast of this research.

There is also a relationship between productivity and relaxing. Getting adequate sleep allows for your body to rejuvenate.[99] Cross-sectional studies from around the world show a consistent increased risk of obesity among short sleepers in children and adults.[100] Sleep deprivation causes a host of problems.

I recently had lunch with a young, hard-working father. He told me that he received two weeks of paid vacation a year, but that he only took one. He was proud of his work ethic. I called a time-out to our conversation right then and there. Taking that time off was essential to keeping himself better rested, and it certainly was important to his family. I made him promise to take off both weeks from then on.

He is far from alone. Each year, Americans fail to take off millions of paid vacation days.[101] Anything or anyone driven too hard will break down. We work to live, not live to work. Nothing can survive being driven 100 percent of the time for extended periods. We need time to relax.

Trey Soup

When I was in high school, I worked at Pizza Pub, a restaurant that once stood near California State University. I loved the job, because I got to hang out with my friends, chat with players on the LA Rams who practiced down the street, and endlessly eat pizza. As a teenager, I had the remarkable ability to eat ten slices of pizza and still lose five pounds. If I washed it down with a Coke, I'd lose a few more.

This ability stayed with me until my late twenties. When I hit thirty, some extra pounds started to appear "out of nowhere," but with a little exercise it came right off. By forty, the party was clearly over. If I looked at a pizza, I would gain ten pounds.

I love to eat, and I love to eat a lot of good, rich food. The problem actually got serious, and at one point I was pushing three hundred pounds. I tried a low-fat fad diet, which ultimately made the problem even worse.

Finally I came to face the reality of "calories in and calories out." If I consumed more calories than I burned, I got fat. If I ate fewer calories than I burned, then I lost weight. It is just math.

When I finally accepted the reality of it all, I stopped wasting time with yo-yo fad diets. I discovered a secret that works for me. Once a week I have a ritual. I cut up peppers, mushrooms, cabbage, broccoli, jalapeno, tomatoes, and onions and put it all into a boiling chicken broth. I then add a mixture of seasonings and spices. I call it "Trey Soup."

I have a rule. I can eat all the Trey Soup I want any time I want. It tastes great, is filling and virtually any nutritionist would say it is healthy. This is not some kind of weird kind of powder or pill. My special pot of vegetable soup helped me lose more than eighty pounds and keep it off.

Whenever I feel like eating pizza, steak, hamburgers, or fries, I just go for it—but first I have a big bowl of my soup, which largely fills me up so I can't overdo it. Trey Soup is my third cornerstone *Do* habit.

Hang On

A few years ago, a television documentary about people who had survived disaster caught my attention. In one episode, a woman was featured who had survived the tidal waves resulting from the 1964 Alaskan earthquake. I was interested in studying the event, so I called the only person I knew from Alaska, Steve McSwain. Steve and I had initially met at a conference in Washington, D.C., and he was helpful in showing me around Alaska.

At the end of our afternoon together, Steve said, "Hey Randall, you need to meet my wife. When she was a little girl she was hit by the tidal waves of the Great Alaska Earthquake!" It was an amazing coincidence, but Steve's wife was the woman I had watched on television who prompted me to go to Alaska in the first place!

Rich Habit #29

Brush Your Teeth

Pride in personal hygiene was measured by comparing those who brushed their teeth with net worth. Millionaires are just 5.2 percent more likely to brush their teeth, as compared with those with a negative net worth.

I met Linda, and she recounted her incredible story as we all drove from Anchorage to Seward to survey the tidal wave sites. After the earthquake, tidal waves came up to her home and began pounding away at the foundation. Her father took the family upstairs, but soon the tidal waves got larger, and they had to climb onto the roof for safety. For the entire cold Alaskan night, her father overcame intense physical strain and literally held onto his family as their house was pounded off the foundation and into trees and other structures.

The entire family was put on the presumed dead list and the survivors were amazed when her family walked into town the next day. Certainly Linda's father was a bona fide hero for keeping his family together on the roof all through the night.

This disaster raises interesting issues. In a threatening situation, most parents would go to physical extremes to protect their children. The remaining question is if we are willing to take the heroic step of addressing the more mundane issues of routine health and fitness?

When it comes to health, no amount of knowledge, philosophy, or intention makes a difference by itself. We can have considerable knowledge about exercising, we can have a firm faith and belief that it works and can even own the very finest gym equipment; however, the waistline will only respond to action.

Discipline and action are the absolute requirements for physical fitness. There are no substitutes and fad diets do not work.[102] I am not a nutritionist, but it seems that any diet that overly restricts the types of food eaten will inevitably become so boring that anyone will eventually drop it. Staying in good physical shape requires attention to just a few basics.

There are simple, fundamental

Rich Habit #30
Keep in Shape

Poor eating habits are ranked as the #1 worst habit.

All Time Worst Habits

Eating poorly	272
Procrastination	250
Lack of exercise	177
Not being on time	119
Worrying	107
Not managing money	65
Smoking	62
Drinking	62
Being lazy	57
Not controlling temper	43

physical laws that cannot be circumvented. Fruits, vegetables, salads, and proteins are healthy. Simple carbohydrates and refined or processed foods are not. One of the simplest and most effective methods for weight control is to drink a large glass of water before every meal.[103]

I might never have the chance to be an "extreme situation" physical hero like Linda McSwain's father, but I do have the chance to be a daily physical hero to my family by keeping healthy. Being healthy affects the way you feel, act, and look, as well as the quality of the role you fulfill as a mom, dad, student, leader, or employee.

Recovery

We should avoid the poisons of smoking, drinking, and drugs.[104] One study shows that members of religious groups who abstain from alcohol altogether actually tend to live longer.[105] Approximately 10 percent of the population is alcoholic, which causes immeasurable misery.[106] Many of the homeless people who come to my class were once successful, and it is obvious that alcohol and the emotional wounds they are trying to mask with alcohol are often at the root of their problems.

Portia Nelson wrote in, *There's a Hole in My Sidewalk* some powerful insights into developing new habits.

> *I walk down the street.*
> *There is a deep hole in the sidewalk. I fall in.*
> *I am lost . . . I am helpless.*
> *It isn't my fault . . .*
> *It takes forever to find a way out.*
> *I walk down the same street.*
> *There is a deep hole in the sidewalk.*
> *I pretend I don't see it.*
> *I fall in again.*
> *I can't believe I am in this same place.*
> *But it isn't my fault.*
>
> *It still takes a long time to get out.*
> *I walk down the same street.*
> *There is a deep hole in the sidewalk. I see it there.*
> *I still fall . . . it's a habit . . . but,*
> *My eyes are open.*
> *I know where I am.*
> *It is my fault.*
> *I get out immediately.*
> *I walk down the same street.*
> *There is a deep hole in the sidewalk. I walk around it.*
> *I walk down another street.*

In the early 1930s a hopeless alcoholic by the name of Bill Wilson discovered certain principles by which he could stay sober. These principles now take the form of the famous 12-Steps program. What is less known is that "Bill W.," as he is more commonly known, almost never got around to writing it.

Rich Habit #31
Keep in Control

Those who drink heavily are 53.9 percent more likely to be in debt and 235 percent more likely to be very unhappy.

With six months of sobriety under his belt, Bill, a New Yorker, found himself in Akron, Ohio, on a fruitless business trip. Disappointed and alone, he found himself pacing the lobby of his hotel eying the hotel bar and the light-hearted throng of customers.

Perhaps one drink wouldn't hurt, he thought. But then another stronger, healthier thought took hold. He just somehow knew that he needed to put his energy into finding another hardcore drunk and to work with him.

Armed with a roll of nickels and the hotel's church directory, Bill made call after call at the pay phone looking for someone he could help. On the twentieth call he found a minister who pointed him to a local doctor who, though once of good standing, was now considered a hopeless alcoholic.

> **Rich Habit #32**
>
> **Don't Go Up In Smoke**
>
> Smokers dominate all categories of low net worth under $100,000. Non-smokers are 258.8 percent more likely to be millionaires.

In his quest to be of service, Bill found Dr. Bob, and together they cofounded Alcoholics Anonymous. A fellowship was born that emphasized the importance of helping others, which has since helped millions.

If you have picked up some unhealthy vices, admit it and get real help. Alcoholics Anonymous is huge because they have discovered a successful formula. Part of my family comes from the Hollywood scene and they can party hard, but Hollywood has an ugly side. Some of my closest friends and family attend these Alcoholics Anonymous meetings daily, even though they have been sober for decades. I respect them for this.

Addiction is a very self-centered world, where one is continually consumed about wants and appetites. Mahatma Gandhi said, "The best way to find yourself is to lose yourself in the service of others." If you are on a path to recovery, make sure your program includes being of service to others.

Enjoy Your View

Ship Shape

Our home and work spaces create the environment for our comfort and productivity. Our surroundings have a big influence on our lives.

Deep sea fishing in the waters off Mexico is awesome. There is nothing like having a giant marlin on the line. But in these close quarters, it can become dirty very quickly. I have noticed how rigorously the ship captains and crew keep the boats clean. In almost no time, they have the automatic habit to immediately wash away any mess and collect all the trash. The boat returns to immaculate condition just a few seconds later.

No matter where we live and no matter how large or small our work space, keeping our environment clean enhances our efficiency and creativity. A cluttered environment brings unnecessary stress and drains energy.[107]

Organized environments satisfy important aesthetic needs. Beauty, form, and balance are essential elements in both personal and business life. Billions of dollars are spent on landscaping, remodeling, relocating, or creating a pleasant environment—and rightly so. A clean and

> **Rich Habit #33**
> **Enjoy the View**
>
> Keeping personal and work space clean and organized is a great habit. Those who have an organized work space have a 2.77 times higher chance of having a very satisfying, romantic life and a 3.4 times higher chance of being

organized home and work area reduces stress. A beautiful view, or a nice painting on the wall, is inspiring and can be a catalyst to creativity.

I know prospective employers who will try to get a peek at a job applicant's car, not because they care about what kind of car it is, but to see if the car is kept clean. They know that those who are in the habit of keeping their car clean tend to keep their work space clean and take pride in their personal environment. They also tend to be more organized and productive.

Our homes may be small or large, and our place of business may be a bench in the garage or a portfolio of major facilities. When it comes to managing our environment, the habit of keeping our space maintained, organized, and clean elevates the quality of our lives and businesses.

Order Comes Intentionally

Over the years, I have worked with a colleague who has offices in Honolulu. We met frequently in his conference room when I consulted on the Bikini Atoll nuclear testing site. During our first meeting, the conference room was somewhat messy. The meeting involved people from all over the world, and we were discussing a particularly important case involving hundreds of millions of dollars. I don't know if it was a fluke or not, but the meeting didn't go well. One consultant got very irritated, and, at several points, the mood got angry.

When we met back in Honolulu for the next meeting, the conference room had been completely altered and looked very nice and organized. When I commented

> **Rich Habit #34**
> **Keep It Clean**
>
> Those who respect their communities and pick up other people's trash are 30.2 percent more likely to earn more than $100,000.

on this, my colleague told me that he'd had his office evaluated by a Feng Shui expert. Feng Shui is an ancient Asian belief system that suggests environmental attributes have a positive or negative impact on life.

Because of this expert, all the piles of documents were gone, everything was tidy, and a small water fountain had been added to one of the corners of the meeting room. I personally do not know much about

Feng Shui practices, but I did immediately recognize that the atmosphere had improved. We had several more meetings in that conference room during the next two years, and all of them were friendly and productive. I don't know if this was a coincidence or not, but I tend to believe that the improved environment had an effect on our attitudes.

According to Feng Shui, which coincides with common sense, a student will study better in a clean dormitory room, people will sleep better in a tidy bedroom, and a chef will prepare dishes more creatively in an organized kitchen. Furthermore, a mechanic will make repairs more efficiently with an organized toolbox, and employees will work more productively in a clean environment. In a sense, it can all be summed up in the old adage, "A place for everything and everything in its place."

I have seen people spend tens of thousands of dollars on professional organizers. Actually, organization is fairly simple. We just pick up an item and put it in one of four places, 1) the trash, 2) a donation pile, 3) a pile of stuff to sell, typically at a garage sale or on the Internet, or 4) for stuff that is actually needed, it must go to a specific place. The criteria for this last category are items that were actually used within the last twelve months. That is the formula for going clutter-free.

New York, New York

One of the best examples of repairing a flawed environment and turning it into something extraordinary lies in the story of New York City.

My first trip to New York was in 1987 with a college buddy of mine. I had heard that New York was dangerous, but as a twenty-eight-year-old, six-foot-three guy from Los Angeles, I wasn't very worried.

I should have been.

On my very first night there, we saw gang violence, prostitution, drug dealers, a robbery, and even a murder. The murder was particularly disturbing as a man stabbed another man right in Times Square with police officers no more than twenty feet away. The bad guy got away. It didn't take me long to come to the conclusion that this place was nuts and I left New York, never really wanting to go back.

Years later, I heard that New York had been revitalized, but I knew

I'd have to see this with my own eyes. It was true; it was one of the most amazing urban reversals ever. Mayor Rudolph Giuliani did the impossible—he cleaned up New York. He did it by cleaning up the outer environment first. Until then, the prevailing attitude had been to focus on the big, largely unseen problems, and let the "little" environmental things go. Giuliani reversed this thinking by focusing on the small but visible things such as graffiti, panhandling, blowing horns, and windshield-cleaning extortionists. Walls were scrubbed clean, petty thieves and panhandlers were uprooted, and gutters and sidewalks were patrolled for trash.

In just a matter of months, the movement gained momentum and city residents began to kick in their own efforts and took more pride in where they lived and worked. Somewhere in their conscious or subconscious minds, the residents of New York realized that as individual citizens they could help create and maintain a better environment. A change for the better no longer appeared to be so overwhelming. When their attitude changed, their habits and environment changed as well.

A similar realization and process was going on in the criminals' minds as well, except that they began to realize that they would get nailed for the little things, so they knew they would get nailed for the big things, too. Crime rates dropped like a rock. Apparently it was cleaning up the little things that mattered.

Add Value

Running Out of Air

The scuba diving around the Bikini Atoll nuclear test sites is amazing because the area is so undisturbed. Once, while coming to the end of my dive, I started my ascent with one thousand pounds of air, just as I was supposed to do.

Then I got distracted. I caught sight of some pretty exciting things, including several poisonous lionfish and some sharks. With all the distractions, I used up the air in my tank faster than normal, and suddenly I was out of air. I was just about to drop my weights and bolt for the surface when my diving buddy handed me his "octopus," an alternative source of air from his tank. Everything was fine, and we calmly went up the side of the reef to the surface.

While I was okay, I will never forget that brief moment when I sucked and got no air. It was a lot like that feeling you get at the restaurant when your credit card is declined and you have no cash. It makes you realize that we take a lot of things for granted, until we run out.

Anyone who says "money does not matter" has never slept under a bridge. Having enough money to pay for basic expenses is a key ingredient to life. In the words of Woodrow Wilson, "No one can worship God or love his neighbor on an empty stomach." Money does matter. Knowing the core habits of money management and budgeting is essential.

Modern-Day Slavery

Slavery is the despicable act of putting people into bondage and forcing them to work for the benefit of another. This practice takes various forms and slavery is alive and well today.

In ancient times, cultures all over the world had a crime called "usury," which meant that one loaned money and charged interest. References to this crime go back to Ancient Greece, Rome, Old Testament times, China, Medieval Europe, Islam, and Vedic texts of India. This was because the lenders understood the powerful effects of interest, whereby they could effectively put their borrowers into perpetual bondage.

What was once considered a crime is now a huge lending industry and a way of life for many. Interest charges may not seem like much, but that is a myth. A typical home loan will mean that the borrower will pay for the house about twice. That means you buy a house for yourself, and then work to buy the equivalent of another house for the bank. Consumer loans and credit card debt are worse.

> ### Rich Habit #35
> ### Find a Job You Like
>
> Of all *Do* habits, "poor career choices" ranked as the worst regret. On the other hand, of all *Do* habits, having a fulfilling career ranked as the number one goal, even ahead of having good health or making money.
>
> #### Greatest *Do* Goals
> #### Category Index
>
> | | |
> |---|---|
> | Have a good career | 164 |
> | Retire | 142 |
> | Be healthy | 120 |
> | Make money | 108 |

It is disturbing to see the remarkably high levels of debt incurred by many families, corporations, and even government. The effects of compounded interest are staggering and its effects are corrosive. Indeed, being in debt is true, modern-day slavery. People must work in drudgery day in and day out, with no end in sight. They are not working for their benefit, but for the benefit of their masters, the lenders.

Many countries have accumulated astounding levels of debt. Greece has been one of the worst. Canada, Brazil, China, the United States, and Australia are not far behind. I find it ironic that the United States abolished one form of slavery in the 1800s, only to wander into another form of slavery about a hundred years later along with a staggering national debt.

A part of the *Do* habits is to understand the corrosive forces of compound interest and to avoid excessive debt. The "Banker's Secret," is to understand this remarkable relationship between time and money, and the power of compounding interest.[108]

It gets a little mathematically complicated, but compound interest means that we pay a percentage of our original loan amount, plus interest on unpaid fees and interest, thus payments are compounded and begin to snowball. It all adds up in astounding ways.

One of the most important lessons that came out of my graduate work at UCLA was an illustration of the power of compounded interest. In history classes, we often hear the story about the American Indians selling the Island of Manhattan for $24 in trinkets.

Putting aside the social issues, if the Indians had taken the $24 in trinkets that they received in 1688 for the Island of Manhattan, and traded and invested to obtain a 7 percent annual return, today they would have about $6 trillion dollars. This is enough money to buy back not only all of Manhattan, but much of the United States.

Bankers know the enormous power of interest. Interest earns profits around the clock, all day and all night. Bankers make money on the golf course, while they sleep and over the weekend. Lenders prey on the typical consumer who must have immediate gratification. The banker makes an attempt to extend credit at every reasonable opportunity.

To apply the Banker's Secret, we must flip the concept around for our benefit. First, we use our resources to create something of value. Whether that is a product or service, we are compensated by

> **Rich Habit #36**
> **Save**
>
> Saving money is romantic. Those who save just 1 percent to 5 percent of their income have 35.0 percent better romantic relationships over those who are in debt or just break even.

the market for both the quality and the effectiveness of its distribution. Then with the earnings, we must control spending and save a portion of the earnings, no matter how small.

Rather than going into bondage and paying interest, we earn interest, appreciation, and dividends through savings and investments. Here is a simple example: When we turn twenty, instead of buying a new car and having a car payment of $350 per month, we instead buy a cheap, used car for cash and invest that money and earn 4 percent interest. This alone would mean having over $1.3 million in the bank when we turn sixty-five. If we earn 5 percent, we would have over $2 million. So which is cooler, having a new car and a continual payment, or being a real millionaire?

Thomas Jefferson said, "Never spend your money before you have it." Those who understand the "Banker's Secret" never allow themselves to become slaves to anyone. They carefully budget their money, reject impulse buying, dislike buying anything on credit, and see paying interest as toxic. They pay off their credit cards every month. If they do borrow at all, it is only for careful, conservative, and limited purposes.

Financial Fitness

The *Do* habits enable us to be productive, and basic productivity means we comply with the laws of money. In George S. Clason's essential classic, *The Richest Man in Babylon,* he sets out Laws of Gold that, like the Laws of Gravity, are universal and unchanging.[109]

If you want to know how to build wealth, I'll tell you right now. You may not like these laws, but they have been proven to work for many generations. Those who comply with the laws of money inevitably become wealthier, no matter how small their earnings.

Save. Save 10 percent of what you earn, even if you are in debt. Reject the urge to spend everything you earn. This way you are continually fattening your wallet or purse. Invest this fund in sensible, secure investments. Most financial disasters I see are the result of overspending, not a lack of earnings.

Be Smart. Be careful before investing in anything that is outside of your specific area of expertise, such as your neighbor's new waffle factory. Stick with investments that you really know, diversify, and don't put all your eggs in one basket.

Insure. Protect against potential risks.

Eliminate Debt. If you are in debt, set aside 20 percent of your earnings to pay toward that debt until it is paid off. Start by paying off the highest interest items first, which are often credit cards.

Cut Costs. Cut out all unnecessary expenses and live on a strict budget of 90 percent of your take-home earnings. If you are in debt, live within 70 percent of your income and pay 20 percent toward repaying debts until it is all paid off. Benjamin Franklin said, "Beware of little expenses. A small leak will sink a great ship."

Budget a portion for a worthy charity or noble cause. Be careful, some phony charities make big claims but really just earn high salaries for the operators. Before you give to a charity, look at its IRS Form 990 or check with an independent charity review.

Benjamin Franklin said, "We may either diminish our wants or augment our means—either will do—the result is the same; and it is for each . . . to decide for himself. If you are idle or sick or poor, however hard it may be to diminish your wants, it will be harder to augment your means. If you are active and prosperous or young or in good health, it may be easier to augment your means than to diminish your wants. But if you are wise, you will do both at the same time . . . and if you are very wise you will do both in such a way as to augment the general happiness of society."

With all these rules, you need to decide things such as, "Do I own my house, or does my house own me?" or "Do I own my car, or does my car own me?" If we find ourselves slaves to our stuff, we need less stuff.

If you are wealthy, then you already know that this is true. If you are not and want to be, then start now. Commitment

---

Rich Habit #37

Don't Gamble It Away

Gambling correlates with a lack of education. Those with limited education are 20.0 percent more likely to gamble, but those with a college degree are 19.7 percent less likely to gamble.

to this financial regimen is mathematically proven to generate authentic wealth.

I'm Feeling Lucky

Frequently, I go to Las Vegas on business. As I have done for many years, I take a taxi from the airport to the hotel. I have made it a habit to ask the cab driver if he has ever met anyone who was going home as a big winner. So far, not a single cab driver has reported that anyone has. A few had won some cash, but had subsequently lost it before they went home.

While I have seen many ads that show off big casino winnings and get rich quick schemes, the casinos lure people in with free drinks. If you lose enough money, they know they have a real sucker and will even give you a free room to keep you there. I have never heard of a single wealthy person who has actually made his or her money this way. Ask yourself, how many people do you know who have become wealthy by gambling or from some other scheme? Las Vegas was not built on winners. The casinos ultimately win. It is just math.

Do habits include doing those things that gradually build authentic wealth. This means that we shun all of the cheesy efforts by those who want to take our money and provide nothing of value in return. Of these efforts, gambling is the most cunning. The key to understanding this phenomenon is the "Gambler's Fallacy." Research shows that many gamblers actually believe in the supernatural forces of luck and fate that defy mathematical odds and logic.[110]

For example, if a coin is tossed ten times resulting in eight heads and two tails, a gambler will actually believe that the next ten tosses will favor tails to "even things out." This is the fallacy. The coin has no memory of the prior ten tosses. The coin is not tied to the past at any level. On every throw, there is a 50–50 chance of landing on heads or tails. Dice, coins, and cards are not somehow mystically tied to the past. The casinos know this, and they know that the odds will always favor them in the long run. A gambler will believe that they somehow have money "invested" in a game, so it is a matter of time until it is returned. In reality, past losses do not change the odds of the game and those odds favor the house.

Taken further, the Gambler's Fallacy would explain how two groups of gamblers with different slot machines could behave. One group's slot machines could be set where the chances of winning were random and had extreme highs and lows, but the long-term effects were inevitably a loss. The second set of slot machines could pay out nothing for several pulls, but then pay out small, positive winnings, guaranteeing a winner in the long run.

Gamblers will actually prefer the first slot machine, even if the logic is explained to them. Gamblers prefer the buzz they get from extreme highs and lows, even over the benefits of logical, slow, and guaranteed returns. They believe that they are entitled to beat the odds. Like any buzz, this high is explained by neurotransmitters that are secreted from the brain.[111]

On top of this, the casinos capitalize on the addicted mind-set, and the fact that an addicted gambler sees a "near win" almost the same as a real win. The non-addicted sees a "near win" as what it is, a loss. On the other hand, casino owners program slot machines, and state lotteries deliberately print scratch-off games with many "near wins" to feed the addicted mind.

Recreational gambling may be okay for some, as long as one never really expects to go home a big winner. It is one thing to play a few games for entertainment, but another to set out to make money or bet the rent money on casino games. Anyone interested in building a solid foundation will replace these poor habits with smart ones.

The Titanic

On April 10, 1914, the largest ship in the world, the *Titanic,* set sail from England for its maiden voyage across the Atlantic Ocean to New York. The ship sailed among enormous hype that the luxury liner was too big to ever sink.

Just five days later, disaster struck. Other ships to the north had stopped for the night because of the risk of icebergs. On the Titanic's more southern course, there was only one iceberg within a forty-mile radius. Despite these miniscule odds, the ship and iceberg were destined to meet. It was a "blue iceberg" where only about five feet peaked above the water level. After it was spotted, the ship was quickly turned and the iceberg scraped along the side, piercing a few small holes. The impact was barely noticed by a few of the passengers and crew.

In spite of this accident, nobody should have died. With any ship, there are lifeboats and other ships that come to the rescue. Another ocean liner, the *Californian,* was stopped for the night only nineteen miles away and within easy eyesight of the *Titanic.* Passengers and the crew of the *Californian* watched the white emergency flares go off on the Titanic, but they weren't sure if the flares were meant to signal an emergency, or if the crew and passengers were firing flares in celebration of the maiden voyage. They watched as the ship appeared to be sailing off into the horizon, but actually the ship was tilting and sinking.

Nevertheless, the crew thought that if the ship really was in trouble, its own crew would have sent a radio message, and no such message had been received. At 11:05 p.m., the *Californian* radioman, Cyril Evans, sent a message, but was abruptly cut off by the Titanic radioman who was frantically communicating with Cape Race. Evans turned off his radio and went to sleep.

On board was J. Bruce Ismay, the chairman and managing director of White Star, the company that owned the *Titanic.* Ismay had a habit of cutting costs, including changing plans and opting for cheaper single hull designs and limiting the number of lifeboats.

There were many factors that lead to the *Titanic* tragedy. Ego, unsafe speed, and poor communication with other ships all contributed. But the predominant cause of the *Titanic* sinking was money and Ismay's habit of cutting costs, thereby threatening safety. Ismay opted for the *Titanic* to carry only enough lifeboats for 1,178 people, which was enough for less than half of the people on board. As a result of this tragedy, only 712 people survived.

One bad habit tends to ripple out to others. Ismay himself shoved his way onto a lifeboat while leaving 2,208 others behind to die. He was hated and hounded for the rest of his life.

When it comes to our own set of *Do* habits, we can learn from the

Titanic. Saving a few dollars at the expense of our basic safety is unwise. Listen to the warnings and never think that we are too big or important to sink. Always put integrity ahead of life itself. In short, we must manage our lives, careers, families, and businesses intelligently and in a way that reconciles with our philosophies and core values.

One Tiny Nibble

Fires, earthquakes, and hurricanes cause huge financial losses every year. One earthquake can split bridges, crumble cities, and shift entire continental plates several feet. Hurricanes can tear apart homes like paper and leave miles of destruction in their path. I was once in the front yard of a house where a landslide had split the house open as easily as you would crack an egg.

Fire departments are on constant alert to the damage that a blaze can cause. News reports will run for days covering the awesome damage caused by a tornado. While these types of disasters result in spectacular damage, they do not even come close to the costs of one of the greatest disasters in the world. The damage done by this disaster is incredible, ruining hundreds, if not thousands, of homes and businesses daily. It destroys fortunes and it's going on right now; but you likely won't find it on tonight's evening news. In fact, this tragic problem could be destroying your finances right now, and you may not know it.

> ### Rich Habit #38
> ### Need or Greed
>
> Money brings happiness only to those whose basic needs are not being met. Statistically, the only income level where there was a correlation between income and happiness was for incomes under $25,000 per year. People who earn less than this tend to be less happy. This may be explained when it is more difficult to be happy when basic needs are not being met. However, for all categories of income of $25,000 to $50,000 a year or more, there is no statistical correlation between annual income and happiness.

It's Termites. Although small and often unnoticed, termites are relentless destroyers. All told, termites cause more than $1 billion in damage each year, year in and year out—far more than all earthquake and tornado damage combined.

There is an average of about thirteen or fourteen termite colonies for every acre of land, which puts about an average of three or four full colonies near every house. The insects have been around for 250 million years, and an individual bug can live up to fifteen years, longer than many animals. For much of her life, the queen will lay an average of one egg every fifteen seconds. With so many mouths to feed, the colonies are always looking for their favorite food—wood. It makes no difference whether or not it is wood from the forest or a house, termites love all forms. Their appetites are large and very destructive. One can often insure one's home and business against storms and fire threats, but generally not against termites. Insurance companies are too smart, because they know that the risk with termites is too great.

Comparable to the ongoing gnawing of termites is the disaster that gnaws away at your financial wealth—debt. Debt is the "termite" that eats away at wealth and prosperity and can lead to financial ruin. There has never been a single instance in history of a bankruptcy occurring without debt, which accumulates slowly, quietly, and inconspicuously.

I once knew a man who had no college education, but had a solid, blue-collar job, a nice home, nice cars, and a pleasant life. Along came a "friend" who offered him the chance to invest and get rich quick. The scheme did not involve any of my friend's areas of interest or experience, but his objective was just to make a lot of money. He borrowed against his house and put all of his equity into the scheme. The rest of the story is a disaster. He lost everything, and, of course, the guy selling the scheme got everything.

Simply stated, money-making schemes make money, but only for those selling the scheme. The "get rich quick" mind-set is inevitably a loser, while the "get rich slow and sure" mind-set actually works.

Plan for Disaster

In 1979, the Three Mile Island nuclear power plant near Harrisburg, Pennsylvania, had a nuclear meltdown as a result of a stuck valve. This was a risk calculated to occur one in 200 million reactor years.

All things considered, that's a pretty reasonable risk and far less than the risk we all take every time we get into a car. Nevertheless, the best-laid plans can go wrong, and in the aftermath, the officials quickly acted, evacuating people and shutting the plant down just as a precaution. Despite being a high profile disaster, nobody died and the majority of people remained living in their homes.

The Three Mile Island incident shows that even the best and most meticulously prepared plans can go wrong, but that does not necessarily mean the end of the world. Being truly financially secure means having contingency plans for these events. Any individual or business that operates "too close to the edge," however, is asking for problems. A solid insurance program is necessary for both individuals and organizations.

Get Off the Train

We all know people who make a lot of money but hate their jobs. Confucius said, "Choose a job you love, and you will never have to work a day in your life."

Right out of college, I pursued business opportunities that were not that interesting to me, but that I thought would make me a pile of money. These did make money but, I was bored because I was not doing what I was really cut out for. I thought that becoming a lawyer would be more interesting so I took the entrance exams, applied, and was admitted into law school.

Classes were to start on the next day, and I was swimming in our pool with my family. I was just drifting around on a raft, wondering if I should really pursue being an attorney. The truth is, I was fascinated with damage economics, even though I had limited experience in the field.

I felt it would be interesting to pursue and pioneer the field. As I floated in the pool, I realized that becoming an attorney would be less risky, but pursuing damage economics would be far more interesting. In a decision that would change my life dramatically, I faxed my resignation to the law school the evening before classes started. Then I pursued what really fascinated me. I didn't set out to make more money, but I chose a field that I genuinely enjoyed.

Sandy Hook

On December 14, 2012, in Newtown, Connecticut, twenty-year old Adam Lanza did the unthinkable. Lanza walked into the Sandy Hook Elementary School and killed twenty children and six adult staff members. The world was stunned.

The crime actually started within Lanza's home where he lived with his mother. The house was a white, two-story, three-thousand-square-foot home with green shutters. It was located atop a two-acre hill in an upscale neighborhood, surrounded by other beautiful homes. Inside, the home was nicely decorated with comfortable chairs and furniture that followed the colonial theme. Books, magazines, and dishes were all in perfect order, as if someone still lived there. If you didn't know where you were, you would think you were in any posh, east-coast house. There was a playhouse and some swings outside, expansive green lawns, and the property backed up to a beautiful, green, wooded area. This was not the typical setting for a horrific crime.

Adam Lanza was a recluse and had moved from his upstairs bedroom down into the basement. As I walked through the house, I noticed that his clothes and cluttered living quarters looked like any typical young man's, except that the signs of his obvious fixation on weapons were located on every level throughout the house. There was a gun safe, shooting equipment, and swords in his upstairs bedroom; gun cleaning rods in the dining room and an assortment of daggers and knives in the basement.

The crime spree started when Lanza walked into the upstairs master bedroom and shot his mother, Nancy Lanza, four times as she lay in her four poster bed. From there, Lanza drove down the long driveway to the street and then to the school, which is now the scene of the nation's worst elementary school shooting.

Like every tragedy, there was irreparable emotional damage. There were also practical questions and one of those questions was what to do with the house, then owned by the bank. At their request, I flew to the headquarters of Hudson City Savings Bank and sat in the boardroom with the bank's top executives to discuss the situation.

I knew that this $37-billion bank was well-known for avoiding the reckless lending in the mid-2000s and that *Forbes* magazine had called it the "best managed bank" during a time when many other banks were falling apart. This preeminent management style was evident when I arrived. The bank executives were clearly focused on the community and doing whatever they could to help. The bank's CEO, Denis Salamone, told me directly that the objective was to simply do what was best for the Newtown community. Though they were a bank, this situation had nothing to do with money.

There was an immediate concern about the status of the property. We quickly decided that the property should be secured and maintained until final decisions could be reached. Furthermore, we felt that it was appropriate to remove and destroy all of the furniture and belongings within the house. A local property manager, Jeff Woerz, carefully oversaw and documented that all of the home's belongings were properly removed and incinerated. The job was so complete, that not a single scrap of paper was left.

In the ensuing weeks, I investigated the fate of properties associated with other tragedies throughout the United States and Europe. After completing my research, I met with the Newtown's Mayor Pat Llonda and the Police Chief Michael Kehoe. There I presented my findings outlining the nine options for handling the Lanza house. We had long, frank conversations about the situation and discussed pros and cons of each option. My only agenda was to express the concern of the bank executives and to set forth comprehensive research, along with the advantages and disadvantages of each option. This information was for the community leaders to consider in their decision. The bank executives and I would respect their judgment, and we would do whatever we could to make it happen.

Ultimately, the community leaders determined the best option for them was to bulldoze the house. The community was sensitive to the families who had lost children, and that house stood as a sad, uncomfortable reminder of those losses. To accommodate the community's request, the bank donated the property to the city.

In economics, we have terms like "highest and best use," "financially feasible," and "maximally productive use," which are all centered on maximizing profits. However, as a sociologist, I know that not every great business decision centers on maximizing dollars. The truly great organizations, even banks, understand that doing what is right always comes before doing what is profitable.

Chapter 16

The Next Step for *Do*

A Common Denominator

L eonardo da Vinci said, "It had long since come to my attention that people of accomplishment rarely sat back and let things happen to them. They went out and happened to things." When we have our act together with our health, finances, and space, we can go to the next level. The pinnacle of *Do* habits is a strong work ethic and a service mind-set.

Walt Disney applied for military service when just sixteen years old, but being underage, his application was rejected. Determined to be of service, he pressed on and joined the Red Cross. As an ambulance driver, he had the habit of drawing sketches and cartoons all over the vehicle and anywhere else, to cheer people up.

St. Francis of Assisi discarded his wealth to live simply and serve others. Audrey Hepburn worked tirelessly in her fight against AIDS. Benjamin Franklin was born into poverty but was a major influence politically, socially, and scientifically. Fredrick Douglas rose above slavery to become an author and abolitionist.

Lincoln had an extraordinary work ethic that he obtained from growing up on a farm, splitting rails for fences, and keeping store at New Salem, Illinois. His law partner said of him, "His ambition was a little engine that knew no rest." Churchill would frequently say that victory came only to those who worked long and hard, and who are willing to pay the price in blood, sweat, and tears.

Houdini had an unstoppable work ethic. He performed his difficult feats with *Do* habits of exercise and mental condition. To develop his capacity for holding his breath, Houdini installed an oversize bathtub in his house so that he could practice regularly. Determined to make every moment productive, while casually chatting with friends, he would habitually perform card and coin tricks without looking at his hands, or tie and untie knots with his feet. Perhaps this was a little distracting for his guests, but it worked for him.

George Washington Carver said, "It is not the style of clothes one wears, neither the kind of automobile one drives, nor the amount of money one has in the bank, that counts. These mean nothing. It is simply service that measures success."

Yogi Berra, the baseball star, never lost sight of the importance of integrity and hard work. Even though he had been recruited to the Yankees' championship team, Yogi worked in the hardware section of Sears Roebuck in the offseason.

The great spiritual, philosophical, and religious figures universally built upon the concept of strong *Do* habits. Moses led his followers out of Egypt and served his people for forty years in the wilderness. Jesus of Nazareth's ministry was entirely focused upon service, helping those in both physical and spiritual need, teaching, and healing the sick. He was so completely devoted to His mission of service that He did not even have a place to call home. Ultimately, He gave His life for humanity.

Buddha taught that to be idle is a short road to death. Muhammad told his followers to feed the hungry and visit a sick person and to assist any oppressed person.

Plato said that the greatest wealth is to live content with little. Aristotle said, "We are what we repeatedly do, excellence is therefore not an act, but a habit!"

Quiet Giants

In her nineties, my mom could be found taking meals to shut-ins and those under hospice care, always much younger than herself. My dad was a fixer. Even in his nineties, he could be found at a neighbor's or friend's house fixing an electrical problem, repairing an appliance, or doing some other project. Both were quiet giants—people who quietly lead great lives.

The opportunities to serve are all around us. Think of a simple trip to the grocery store. Picture yourself driving courteously, allowing other drivers to change lanes in front of you. On the way in, you pick up a piece of trash on the ground. In the store, you help a struggling elderly woman load a heavy item into her cart and assist a young mother to reach an item on the top shelf. At the checkout line, picture yourself allowing a rushed customer to cut in line ahead of you. Opportunities to serve are everywhere.

Perhaps we won't have the opportunity in our lifetime to perform an act of service that garners worldwide attention like Gandhi or Mother Teresa. But that's not the point. The most selfless acts of service can be offered quietly and with no spotlight. Being a person of value and leading a rich life transcends what people see on the outside.

Perhaps the most important place we can be of service is at home and in our own communities. Love is more than a feeling, love is an action. Only by taking action and serving others can we show our love. We all have an opportunity to be great neighbors. I've been fortunate enough to have lived in neighborhoods where neighbors reached out to make my family feel welcome. If this is not happening in your neighborhood, it can, and it can start with you. Start a progressive dinner with your neighbors, take some cookies next door, mow a lawn or wash a car of the elderly person across the street, or host a Ping Pong tournament. Just do something. Finding opportunities for service is simply a matter of putting down the remote and looking around. Not once have any of the causes I've been affiliated with turned away volunteers because they had enough.

The Ultimate Buzz

I admit it. I like my adrenalin buzzes. I have traveled to fifty states and have explored all seven continents. I have sky dived, hiked mountains, water skied, jet skied, and driven race cars. I have flown planes and helicopters, and have ridden in hot air balloons over migrating herds in Africa's Serengeti. I have come face-to-face with lions and have been stalked by crocodiles. On many occasions, I have gone scuba diving in shark infested waters. I have, in younger years, skied straight down black diamond runs. Several times I have been on live, national television. Most importantly, I was at Led Zeppelin's last concert in Los Angeles.

I don't share any of this to impress you, I share this to *impress upon you* that I know what I'm talking about when I say that the ultimate buzz does not come from any of this. The ultimate *Do* habit is to be of service, which is the best buzz of all. Arthur Ashe said, "From what we get, we can make a living; what we give, however, makes a life."

Celebrities and the super rich often go to remarkably expensive drug rehabilitation facilities, only to relapse. This is because only a part of the problem was addressed. While they are able to chemically detoxify, they remain self-absorbed. Addiction is the quintessential phenomena of self-absorption where one is constantly focused upon oneself and one's cravings. Even after treatment, their focus remains inward. Indeed, people who are addicted are virtually obsessed with themselves and how they feel and what they want. While the *Me* cornerstone is important, addicted people tend to be chronically stuck there.

Service cures this toxicity. It takes people from thinking about themselves to thinking of others. It is the most powerful drug there is. It can cure even the hardest core addict where everything else fails.

If you are wallowing in your problems, go find someone who is worse off. Got a health problem? Just go to a children's hospital and hang out with a seven-year-old child with terminal cancer. Got a money problem? Go serve food at a kitchen for the homeless. Got relationship problems? Go help battered women at a shelter. Have a difficult child? Go to a children's mental health ward. Feeling depressed? Sit down and talk to a crack addict. Really, get out there. I don't care where you live, you won't have to go far to find any of these. They are right down the street from where you live.

The greatest buzz comes from helping someone and getting a "helper's high."[113] Sitting down with someone who is desperate and hurting, and helping them feel a bit better is the best buzz in the world. So, go get buzzed!

The *Do* Challenge Coin

This is where you accept the challenge coin and take responsibility for your own *Do* cornerstone. This is where you do something to build productivity; specifically, get physical, enjoy your view, and add value.

Avoid the January 4th effect. Pick only one new *Do* habit and make it simple. For example, don't commit to doing fifty pushups a day. Rather, commit to doing one, but more if you choose to.

Commit to mastering your new *Do* habit and make it a solid cornerstone of your life. Here are some suggestions, or come up with one of your own:

- Sleep for _____ hours every night.
- Keep a food log.
- Drink _____ glasses of water every day.
- Cut out eating _____ [e.g., fried foods, refined sugar].
- Limit eating to _____ calories per day.
- Cut out drinking _____ [e.g., soda, alcohol, coffee].
- Exercise _____ minutes _____ times per week.
- Spend ___ minutes every night straightening the house or office desk.
- Make the bed every morning.
- Get a physical checkup every _____ .
- Spend _____ minutes cleaning up every day.
- Donate _____ items you don't need every month.
- Save _____ percent of gross income.
- Pay off $ _____ of debt every week.
- Find a new job you enjoy.
- Give up gambling.
- Volunteer in your community _____ hours per month.
- Contribute $ _____ every month to your favorite charity.
- Spend _____ hours every week helping out around the house.

SECTION 4
THE *BE* CORNERSTONE

On good days we live,
on bad days we learn

Chapter 17
The *Be* Habits

The Final Cornerstone

The fourth and final cornerstone is *Be,* which is based on the Latin term *ab aeterno,* meaning *of the eternities.* With the third cornerstone of *Do* habits, we create "to do" lists to manage our health, money, and space; however, we are not *human doings,* we are human beings. With this final cornerstone, we *Be* and create "to be" lists. Here we use our time to create something timeless and build our personal legacy.

> ### The *Be* Cornerstone
>
> The fourth cornerstone *Be* is to use our time to continually progress.
>
> To construct this cornerstone, set clear, written goals, manage time, and record your progress.

Within many great buildings there are time capsules. They can be anything from carvings, statues, art, or buried information for future generations. Similarly, with *Be* habits we fill our personal time capsules with accomplishments that will be of considerable value in the future. Our time capsules can include art we created, music we played, designs we made, photos we took, organizations we helped to build, children we raised, or journals we wrote.

We are all beneficiaries of the others who came before us. Each of us has a heritage to build upon. There are parents, grandparents, mentors, and veterans who helped shape our lives. With the *Be* habits, we add our contributions to those of our predecessors. This is our opportunity to establish a legacy for our successors.

A Trip to the Zoo

As a child, I watched in awe at man's first moon landing. I vividly recall the invention of the handheld calculator and the micro-computer. I have seen television go from black and white tubes in big wooden boxes, to color and now screens that are huge and flat. Every morning I read my favorite Dick Tracy cartoons in the *Los Angeles Times* and got a chuckle from the outrageous, futuristic notion that Detective Tracy had a two-way wrist communicator that allowed him to see and talk with others. Today, many of us carry around a smartphone that blows away Tracy's special watch.

> **Rich Habit #39**
> **Get Out There**
>
> Of all *Be* habits, travel ranked as the #1 goal.

In 1903, the Wright brothers were the first to fly, and it lasted only twelve seconds. Just sixty-six years later, man landed on the moon. As a child, I talked to my grandfather about the transition he witnessed from horse and buggies to the automobile. In one lifetime, mankind has cured polio, taken transcontinental travel from many months to mere hours, gone from small buildings to skyscrapers and begun to contemplate trips to other planets.

When I was in kindergarten, my parents took me to the zoo. I still remember staring eye-to-eye with monkeys and feeling a sense of wonder at the size of the elephants and fright as I watched the snakes slither in their cages. I was simply astounded to actually see all of these animals I had only seen in books and magazines, or on television.

The *Be* habits are distinct from the first three. The animal kingdom addresses the first three habits. Animals have *Me* habits to think and learn at some level. Animals are social creatures and have *We* habits as they live together as a school or pack. Certainly all wild animals are productive with *Do* habits and establish homes, dens, or nests and collect food. However, when I take my own children to the zoo, the elephants, monkeys, and snakes are doing the exact same things they were doing when I was in kindergarten. In fact, they are doing the exact same things they have been doing for thousands of years.

Of course, people do many of the same things we did thousands of years ago, but people are distinct from the animal kingdom because of the *Be* habits. People set goals, strategize, and progress. *Progression* is the essence of the *Be* habits. The *Be* habits are our opportunity to set goals, manage our time, and make our personal mark.

Creating a legacy does not need to be complicated. One legacy I remember well was that of a man named Bill White. For a little boy with the attention span of a goldfish, sitting through church could be painful. But Bill always brought a brown paper bag full of candy and passed it out to the children after the service. He had a contagious smile, loved to joke around, and somehow made it all fun. It was a simple thing, but to this day everyone smiles when Bill White's name comes up.

Pick a Target

Inspired by a study by University of North Carolina professor Dr. Gerald Bell, my research staff and I asked thousands of retired executives, "If you could live your life all over, what would you do the same?" Their answers provide valuable insights into priorities.

Retired Executives:
"What would you do the same?"

1. Marriage	• I would marry the same person all over again. • I would marry the same spouse; we had a great family. • I stayed married to my late spouse for more than fifty years.
2. Career	• I worked for a great company for most of my career. • I would still teach in spite of the low salary.
3. Education	• I obtained all the education I could pay for, or beg, borrow, or steal. • I am a life-long learner.

- I decided to go to college when it was discouraged.

4. Children & Family
- I raised my children with love and set a good example for them.
- I spent a lot of time with my son/daughter and coached him/her in his/her sports.
- I have beautiful adult children.

5. Spiritual
- The main goal of my life was to be spiritual.
- I stayed an active member of my church.
- I prayed.
- I adopted animals needing loving homes.
- I volunteered to help the addicted and afflicted.
- I cared about the environment.

6. Travel & Hobbies
- I made time for my wife and family
- Traveled and saw the world.
- We had fun in the outdoors.

7. Self-Development
- I always went by my motto of "do the right thing."
- Even the "bad stuff" has been a learning opportunity and a springboard to development.
- I maintained my positive attitude.
- I kept my self-respect.

8. Friendships
- Directly helped financially and emotionally friends and acquaintances in need.
- I developed lifelong friends.

9. Money
- I worked hard and saved so I could have a nice retirement.

10. Health
- I take care of my health.
- I stopped smoking in my twenties.
- I am physically active.

We also asked these retired executives, "If you could live your life all over again, what would you do differently" About 9 percent of the respondents had major regrets and said that they would do everything differently:

**Retired Executives:
"What would you do differently?"**

1. Education
- I would have studied harder in school.
- I would have finished my college education.

2. Career
- I would have left my corporate world and started my own business sooner.
- I would have followed my passion for the arts.

3. Marriage
- I would not have tried to change my spouse's outlook.
- I would have helped more around the house.
- I would have tried to understand my former spouse and possibly stay together.

4. Children & Family
- I would have spent less time at my job and more time with my kids.
- I would never have had children to try and save my marriage.
- I would have stood up to my parents.
- I would have spent more time with my grandkids.

5. Money
- I would have invested more of my income for a better retirement.
- I should have banked some of the money I squandered throughout the years.

6. Self-Development
- I would have had more ambition.
- I would take one day as it comes and not look so far into the future.

	• I would have had a better sense of humor.
	• Be much less concerned about doing things right or what people might think.
7. Spiritual	• Perhaps I would have devoted more time to God and my spiritual health.
	• I would have changed religions sooner.
	• I would have made religion a priority earlier in life.
	• I would have started helping needy people sooner in life than I did. Helping needy people gives you a very good feeling inside.
8. Health	• I would have eaten less.
	• I would have kept my alcohol consumption under control.
	• I never would have started smoking.
9. Travel & Hobbies	• I would have been more adventuresome.
•	I would have learned to read music.
10. Relationships	• I would have avoided the mistake of expecting others to "do the right thing."
	• I would listen more carefully, thank people, and appreciate people more.

These retired executives provide some important insights. First, the top four categories are consistently education, marriage, children and family, and career. Clearly these four areas are a driving force in life and happiness. When marriage and children and family are combined, this category taken together easily trumps all others areas in both studies.

This study gives us the benefit of hindsight from thousands who were successful, at least by job title. Also, I noticed that not a single executive expressed that more time would have been spent in the office.

A Life Well Lived

"A Life Well Lived" is the inscription on the grave on one of the greatest men I have ever known: my dad. Preston Bernhisel Bell left a great legacy. He was a terrific man, but he never took himself too seriously. He used to say

> *I never run when I can walk.*
> *I never walk when I can sit.*
> *I never sit when I can lie down.*
> *And . . . I always eat when food is offered.*

What made this quote amusing was that my dad was actually the hardest worker I've ever known. If someone needed a helping hand, day or night, my dad was right there. My dad taught us through his example that the greatest joy did not come through selfish consumption, but through service to others. When my dad passed away, I realized that I had spent the first half of my life getting. Now I wanted to be more like him—I want to spend the second half giving.

My dad worked as a mechanical engineer for Fender, which makes guitars used by many famous musicians. One day he brought home an old work bench that the company had thrown out when modernizing the factory. It was an original used from the days of Leo Fender himself.

That old workbench sat in our garage for years and provided many opportunities for practical intelligence. On it we built book shelves, worked on school science experiments, and made model airplanes.

A parade of rock stars had come through the Fender plant; my dad would talk about how he had worked with them and engineered their guitars. We would talk about how that bench might have been used to fix Jimmy Hendrix or Keith Richards Stratocaster guitar, or even Jimmy Page's Telecaster.

Today, my dad's old workbench is in my garage, and I think about his legacy as I work on my projects. My mom and dad knew that contributing to the community brought about a sense of belonging and satisfaction. My parents were great examples of hard work, service, and charity that provided a great legacy to their posterity. Their traditional values are not obsolete. Indeed, they are needed more today than ever.

I tell my children, "I want you to be happy and successful, but mostly happy." Joy is not for the hereafter, it is for the here and now. Joy is that deep feeling of happiness and contentment in knowing that a job is well done and that we made a contribution. We get joy from setting goals, using our time wisely, and establishing our own unique personal legacy. The *Be* habits facilitate this growth.

Chapter 18
Pick a Target

A Sense of Legacy

I love England. I love the culture, architecture, and history. To me, there is no sight more beautiful than the rolling green English countryside and grazing sheep, or the energy and movement of its great towns and cities. I connect with the history that is everywhere, from the Big Ben clock on the House of Parliament to the obscure cobblestone alley. I love the smells when I walk in from the cold into a warm fish-n-chip shop. I enjoy the sense of heritage and the accents of red phone kiosks, postal pill boxes, and double-decker buses that are scattered everywhere. I love the jolly laughter of English men and women as I tell them that my Californian accent is the purest form of English!

I am drawn to the United Kingdom because it is the land of my ancestors. I am moved as I retrace their steps where each generation built upon the accomplishments of the last.

When I am in London, I usually take time to visit Westminster Abbey, which to me is the world's finest cathedral. It is the final resting place for kings and queens, as well as statesmen, scientists, poets, and writers. Here we find memorials for Shakespeare, Longfellow, Churchill, and Dickens. I am always moved by its most prominent grave, which is located near the front entrance and is the one spot always circled by flowers. In part, the inscription reads:

> Beneath this stone rests the body
> Of a British warrior,

Unknown by name or rank,
Brought from France to lie among
The most illustrious of the land . . .
Gave the most that man can give
Life itself
For God,
For King and Country,
For loved ones home, and empire
For the sacred cause of justice and
The freedom of the world
They buried him among the kings because he
Had done good toward God and toward
His house.

Creating a legacy means that we contribute to a cause greater than ourselves. This soldier, as fallen soldiers everywhere, have left a noble legacy and each has given us a gift of freedom. Their lives had purpose. They made their mark.

It has struck me that the man buried in the most prominent spot within this huge cathedral is a man whose name we do not know. We do not need to inherit a giant monarchy or make a great discovery in order to create an important legacy; we do need to contribute to a cause that is greater than ourselves. I am convinced that many of our greatest heroes, and many of the world's greatest accomplishments, belong to people whose names we do not know.

Sadly, some have no vision and squander their time and freedom to indulge in acquiring stuff or in some other trivial pursuit, only one day to realize that their lives are about over and had no meaning. Of course they will have reasons. However, bad behavior with a reason has a name. It is called "bad behavior."

On the other hand, the *Be* habits are not about building trivial pursuits, they are about great pursuits. Those who are creating a legacy do not shove others around to grab what they want. They are less interested in the enticing trilogy of property, prominence, and power.

They care for others. They put others' interests in front of their own. They are productive and industrious. They have clear and deliberate goals.

Turning It Around

At the time of the Los Angeles Riots in 1992, I was living in Santa Monica, just west of Los Angeles. Initially, I was not very concerned, as we were miles from the epicenter of the violence.

Curfews had been imposed, so we primarily stayed in our apartment. As the riots heated up, it looked as though we might need to stay inside for a while. Since all the restaurants were closed, I went to the supermarket to stock up on some groceries.

When I got to the supermarket, I realized that I was not the only one with this idea. The market had not received any deliveries in days, and there were crowds of people buying anything in sight. I was surprised to see that the shelves were nearly empty, and the good foods were long gone. All that remained was stuff I'd never heard of. Looking over my options, I bought some canned baked yams and sugared beets. Then I got in the checkout line, which extended all the way to the back wall of the store.

When I got back to the apartment, the news showed that the riots were spreading rapidly. The area was looking like a war zone. Many roads were blocked, and I finally realized that we were utterly trapped with a burning police zone on one side and the ocean on the other. We had just a little food and no protection. I was starting to get concerned.

When the riots finally stopped and the smoke settled, the riots had spread to 21st Street, just eleven blocks away. Clearly, I had been negligent in preparing for an emergency. For years I had intended to get an emergency preparedness pack put together but, "the road to hell is paved with good intentions."

Setbacks do not have to be negative. They can be good for us. A setback causes change and prompts new action. Change wakes us up to senses and aspirations that may have gone dormant. Vince Lombardi once said, "In great attempts, it is glorious even to fail." Clearly I had failed to heed the warnings to prepare for an emergency. Today, I am happy that I learned from the experience and am now prepared.

Nobody can become who or what they want to be by remaining where they are. We all have areas that need improvement, and that is why we all need to set goals. Some don't set goals because they believe that they are too busy or do not have the time. However, if something will take five years to achieve, that time will go by, whether the goal is completed or not. If getting a college degree or a master's degree will take two or four years, that time will go by whether or not one goes back to school.

Goals are the vehicle to take us from where we are to where we want to be.

Goal Setting

If you place fleas in a jar, they will jump right out. If you put a lid on the jar, the fleas will jump and hit the lid, but after a while they will jump only high enough that they do not hit the lid at all.[114] Their failure has conditioned them. Eventually, you can take the lid off, and while they are perfectly capable of jumping right out, their prior conditioning prevents them from doing so. This "conditioning to failure" affects people too. Goal setting breaks through this mind-set and takes us to places that we didn't think were possible.

Before we set goals, we might first take a sober look at our priorities, the people in our lives, as well as our level of productivity in relation to what we want. A *Me We Do Be* assessment identifies our weak spots and lays the foundation for genuine development.

When setting a real goal, one can first examine the basis for that goal by asking the following questions: Is this really "my" goal, or is it being

> **Rich Habit #40**
> **Pick a Target**
>
> Goal setting has a range of benefits. Those who have clear, written goals are 74.9 percent more likely to have a very satisfying romantic life as opposed to those who have no clear goals. The data suggests that those with a clear sense of direction are simply more appealing.

done for someone else? Does the goal compatible with my philosophical core values? Is the goal fair to all involved? Is the goal consistent with other goals? How will life or business specifically benefit from this goal? From there, the goal-setting process can truly begin.

The first step is to list all of your potential goals. Then, review the list and prioritize the most important ones. Deliberately choose the top goal—the one that is of utmost importance. Commit the goal to writing. Writing down goals transforms a good intention into a real objective. It defines the future and commits one to action.

With your goal established, list all the obstacles to achieving it, along with the related tasks. Most goals cannot be accomplished alone, so list all the people whose help you might need. Share your goal with others who have your best interests at heart. Use caution, as some "move up" goals should not be shared with anyone who may be intimidated by your reaching it, such as some coworkers or even superiors at work. They may not share your enthusiasm when your achievement could be perceived as leaving them in the dust!

Break the goal up into small steps and prioritize each step, then establish deadlines for each step. Start working the plan, and be persistent. Consistent and relentless effort has an awesome power.

Brainstorming

In many situations where we are setting goals or want to elevate, brainstorming can be a great tool. Brainstorming is a process where the individual or group addresses a problem and then simply lists every idea or potential solution that comes to mind.

There are some basic components to brainstorming successfully. First, the problem must be adequately defined and ideas for solutions need to be offered, but the session must be a genuine free-for-all, where anything goes.

As ideas are gathered, there should be absolutely no evaluation, criticisms, or comments. The idea is to create an atmosphere where it is safe to say anything, be creative, and think of out-of-bounds ideas. All ideas can be catalysts to real solutions. A designated scribe can be appointed to write everything down.

Once every idea has been presented, they can then be sorted and the pros and cons can be considered. No idea should be tossed out until it is seriously considered. What might sound ridiculous on the front end can be a genuine stroke of genius once it's given a fair chance. Ultimately, the best solutions will rise to the top.

A Snake Bite

Once I consulted on a case that took me to the most remote place on planet Earth, the tiny island of Utrik, which was dusted with radioactive fallout after nuclear tests on the nearby Bikini Atoll.

When you spend a week on a remote island that has no running water, no electricity, and no cell service, you have a lot of time to talk and meditate. I met a medical doctor who was from Malaysia, and we talked for hours and hours.

Late one night, he told me a story that had clearly haunted him for years. As a young doctor right out of medical school, he treated a patient who had been bitten by one of the area's poisonous snakes. He followed the procedures as outlined in his textbook, which stated that snake bite victims should be injected with a vial of anti-venom. He did this, but to his dismay, the patent did not recover. The patient died.

My new doctor friend told of the grief of losing this patient and having to tell his family. Later he learned that to successfully treat a snake bite victim, he needed to not only inject the patient with anti-venom, but continue the injections every hour until the patient's symptoms subsided. He agonized that if he had only known this, he was certain that he could have saved the patient.

I listened to him as he relived the entire experience and the grief and guilt that he had carried for years. When he had nothing else to say, we just sat there for a while, silently looking at the silhouette of the palm trees and the moon hovering over the lagoon.

After a long while, I spoke. I told my friend that I was sorry about this horrible event. I told him that this must have been a burden to carry around. However, I was impressed with his high level of service. It was clear that he had entered the medical field for the right reasons, and that was to be of service and help others. I was impressed that he had remembered and followed his training, and that he did everything he knew to try to save this man. I was impressed that he went the extra mile to later investigate what went wrong. He did what his training told him to do. His actions were not faulty. His heart had been in the right place.

After sharing these thoughts with him, we then talked about how to take some of the negative energy he was still feeling about this tragedy and do something positive. Not only could he tell all of his colleagues about the flaw in the textbook, but he could share this information with the medical professors. He could broadcast this information far and wide to new medical students. He could contact the publisher of the textbook and inform them of the flaw. He could be of great service to the medical community by exposing the problem and promoting the advanced knowledge he had gained. He could literally save lives.

A smile came over his face as his new goal came into focus, and he started to eagerly plot his strategy for getting the word out when he returned home.

Carrying around negative energy is like a ball and chain. It just wears us out. Negative energy is anything that causes guilt, shame, embarrassment, regret, or lingering anger. We can feel this negative energy for any unresolved problems, even those that were not our fault. We feel this negativity because the situation has never been resolved, and it needs to be.

We can indeed resolve anything that generates this negative energy by making a choice to do something positive with it. We can set a goal of resolution. We can talk to others, apologize, forgive, sever toxic relationships, educate others, or contribute to a worthy cause.

Our Personal Best

Everyone is in the business of problem solving. The computer industry exists to solve data management and communication problems, the auto industry exists to solve transportation needs, and the medical industry exists to solve medical problems. Homemakers solve the challenges of running a household. Students must solve problems to complete their homework.

Whatever and wherever the case, problems should be viewed with an attitude of facing a challenge rather than avoiding it. A colleague of mine noted that the small problems never made him any money, but he welcomed big problems because they were profitable.

I once had the chance to chat with one of my all-time heroes, John Wooden. Wooden was not only an outstanding basketball player, but also the world's finest basketball coach; he led his UCLA team to an unprecedented ten national championships.

One of the most powerful developmental mind-sets is what I call "The Wooden Approach," as opposed to the "score-driven" perspective.[115]

John Wooden sets out to "do one's personal best," while the score mind-set sets out to "win a championship." The score mind-set is obvious and a quick sell, but Wooden's approach sets out a loftier goal and is ultimately more effective.[116]

Many focus on the score and winning, while the Wooden Approach focuses on one's self-development and the maximization of one's capabilities. In our world, the masses are generally "score driven." These individuals and organizations focus singularly on the score, as a measurement for success. With this as their focus, the required attributes for building genuine value can be swept aside in the relentless and often elusive goal of capturing the all-important score.

On the other hand, the game-driven are problem solvers who focus on maximizing their potential and playing the game to the best of their ability. It is not that they are unaware of the score, but their heads are truly into the game. They love to create value and they enjoy developing a great strategy. Ironically, success is the natural result of this approach, yet it is not directly pursued. Abraham Lincoln said, "I can do the very best I know how—the very best I can; and I mean to keep on doing so until the end."

It is not a matter of what is accomplished, but what could have been accomplished had things been done correctly. Walt Disney said, "Get a good idea and stay with it. Dog it and work at it until it's done, and done right." General George S. Patton said, "If a man has done his best, what else is there?"

Chapter 19

Operational

Make It Happen

It's About Time

To build a legacy, we must use our time wisely. Time management is the difference between taking charge and being proactive, or just being reactive to everything around us. Here we ask if our tasks are prioritized and if our days are organized. Within our organizations, we ask if our systems, operations, and meetings are well-planned and effective. Managing our time might seem like an overwhelming task, but as Abraham Lincoln said, "The best thing about the future is that it comes only one day at a time." Time is a highly valuable and non-replaceable commodity and it is our choice to spend it wisely or squander it.

> ### Rich Habit #41
> ### Check the Time
> Those who maintain both a calendar and to-do list are 289.3 percent more likely to be millionaires, as compared with those who have no real set schedule.

The rules of time management begin with following the advice of the Dalai Lama, who says, "Spend some time alone every day." Fifteen minutes of planning increases efficiency 25 percent to 50 percent for the next twenty-four hours.[117] When I get into the office each morning, I immediately sit down and plan out my day in writing. It is a simple process, but my day is far more productive because of it.

Use part of your planning time to write down everything that you want to accomplish that day. Remember that every time you think "I've got to remember . . ." it causes the same kind of stress as trying to wake up on time without an alarm clock.[118] Writing things down relieves this type of stress.

Prioritize your list of things to do. Often the first thing you do sets the tone for the rest of the day. So, take the absolute must do items and place a dot or an A by them. Then, place a B by the items you would like to do and a "C" by the things that are not a high priority. One tip is to circle all the tasks that require a trip, so that you can bundle these tasks into only one trip.[119]

Do the most difficult tasks first so that you don't drain your mental energy during the day worrying about them. As someone once said, "It's best to eat the biggest frog first." Items of personal daily discipline, such as exercise and reading, should not be placed on tomorrow's list.

Once our day is planned, then we just make it happen. Remember, "The harder I work, the luckier I get." Things just seem to go smoother. Success comes from putting priorities into action. As you accomplish the tasks on your list, check them off. The action of checking off completed tasks is physiologically satisfying.[120]

Ready, Shoot, Aim!

The use of our time is a blend of science and art. The science is to set priorities and get things done. The art is to be flexible and finding that sweet spot somewhere between patience and procrastinating.

Hope is not a strategy. It takes action and a logical day-to-day plan. It takes persistence and patience to steadily build something of value. Behavioral studies show that truly great achievements were typically preceded with about ten thousand hours of effort.[121] That's about five years of a full-time effort.

The baseball player Yogi Bear was famous for saying, "If you don't know where you are going, you may end up there." Life is what is happening while we are making other plans. Achievers avoid putting a priority off until the twelfth of never.

Those who are successful in creating a meaningful legacy have a strong sense of priority mixed with action. They see the big picture. They skip over all the noise and distraction while they pursue their objective and capitalize on their talents.

One day I had lunch with Dick Leach, one of the greatest tennis coaches in history. His son, Rick, won Wimbledon, as did his is daughter-in-law, Lindsey Davenport. This guy loves tennis. I asked Dick what it took to be a champion. He told me that there were simply two ingredients for championship players: talent and work.

Dick explained that he had met a lot of tennis players who had the gift of raw talent. But they lacked the work ethic, daily discipline, and passion to achieve champion status. They did pretty well on their talent, but they would never reach the top. On the other hand, there were players who were passionate, worked hard, and did everything asked of them and more. They also did well, but frankly they lacked the natural talent to achieve champion status. It was clear: when a player has both the gift of talent and puts in the hard work, championship is achieved.

> **Rich Habit #42**
> **Use Time Wisely**
>
> Being on time ranked number one of all *Be* habits people are most proud of, while the number one regret of all *Be* habits, was wasting time.

Sociological research backs up this concept. We all have a talent. I wish mine were tennis, but it is not. However, we all have the blood of a champion of something pumping through our veins. We take whatever talent we have and then we make it a priority. We put in the time. We practice, we push, and we act. By taking our gift of talent and combining it with our own hard work, we can become champions in whatever our particular gift is.

The Atom Bomb

On August 6, 1945, General Paul Tibbets was flying the B-29 bomber "Enola Gay" as he dropped the atomic bomb Little Boy on Hiroshima, Japan. It was the first wartime nuclear strike in world history. This uranium atomic bomb was untested, yet the war effort was so urgent that it went forward.

Hiroshima had been chosen as a target because it was an industrial city that had an important role in the war effort. At that time, the city had not been bombed, so it would be clear for the Japanese to see the net devastation of this new weapon.[122]

The bomb was largely ineffective in that less than 2 percent of the radioactive material actually detonated. Yet the blast equaled 16 kilotons of TNT and destroyed everything for a one-mile radius. It killed more than one hundred thousand people and destroyed about 70 percent of the city.[123] When I visited Hiroshima, I saw areas where the flash was so intense that it literally burned shadows into the stonework.

When I consulted for the Nuclear Claims Tribunal, I had the opportunity to meet General Tibbets. As I often do with research trips, I took one of my children with me and this time it was my oldest son. General Tibbets told us that when the bomb went off the blast was so bright he saw the bones of his hands as they covered his face. My son asked him what it felt like and the General replied that it felt like a "good spanking."

I was a little surprised when my son then asked General Tibbets if he regretted dropping the bomb. General Tibbets looked my son right in the eye and said that no, he had no regrets whatsoever. We had not started the war and the General told my son that he had seen films showing what the Japanese had done to our soldiers. The war needed to end and he was anxious to do whatever needed to be done to end it.

Despite the bomb's stunning effect, today's Hiroshima stands in stark contrast to the sites of many major disasters I've researched. For example, I was invited to lecture at a conference in South America and I noted areas that, after decades, were still damaged by the great Chilean earthquake in 1960. Not so for Hiroshima. It is a completely developed, clean, and efficient city. There are no remnants of the damage. The only physical reminder of that fateful day is the Hiroshima Peace Memorial complex and museum that centers on the famous Atomic Bomb Dome, a former industrial facility near the target of the explosion.

A skeleton of the building remains today, which is the focal point of the large complex. An enclosed bridge links two identical buildings that serve as a modern convention center and the museum. In fact, when I was walking to the museum, I accidentally walked to the wrong end and into a shoe convention. Even this complex is a reminder of moving forward. On one end, visitors come to view exhibits related to the bomb, while just yards away, other people come to attend various business conventions. To me, this was symbolic of looking to the lessons of the past, while also looking to the business of going forward.

The people of Hiroshima were dealt an unprecedented blow. Yet they addressed their mistakes and their problems and moved forward. One of the most fascinating aspects of Hiroshima was that rebuilding efforts were started just two days after the bomb had been dropped.[124]

The people of Hiroshima literally had an atom bomb dropped on them but walking the streets today, one would never know. Not only are the streets of Hiroshima beautiful, but Japan has risen to be a great, peaceful nation.

A paced, day-to-day effort is a valuable virtue that allows one to not just return to one's pre-tragedy baseline, but actually to overcome and create an even higher level of prosperity.

Make It Happen

For centuries, many emphasized the avoidance of the "Seven Deadly Sins" of pride, envy, gluttony, lust, anger, greed, and sloth. Around 1730, while in his late twenties, Benjamin Franklin took a positive view and rather than worrying about what not to do he listed thirteen virtues that he wanted to proactively pursue in his everyday activities.[125]

Franklin placed each of the virtues on a separate page of a small book and focused on one virtue for a full week. He evaluated his performance daily. These virtues can be of benefit as we contemplate our own goals:

Benjamin Franklin's 13 Virtues

Temperance: Eat not to dullness; drink not to elevation.

Silence: Speak not but what may benefit others or yourself; avoid trifling conversation.

Order:	Let all your things have their places; let each part of your business have its time.
Resolution:	Resolve to perform what you ought; perform without fail what you resolve.
Frugality:	Make no expense but to do good to others or yourself; i.e., waste nothing.
Industry:	Lose no time; be always employed in something useful; cut off all unnecessary actions.
Sincerity:	Use no hurtful deceit; think innocently and justly, and, if you speak, speak accordingly.
Justice:	Wrong none by doing injuries, or omitting the benefits that are your duty.
Moderation:	Avoid extremes; forbear resenting injuries so much as you think they deserve.
Cleanliness:	Tolerate no uncleanliness in body, clothes, or habitation.
Tranquility:	Be not disturbed at trifles, or at accidents common or unavoidable.
Chastity:	Rarely use venery [pursuit of romantic pleasure] but for health or offspring, never to dullness, weakness, or the injury of your own or another's peace or reputation.
Humility:	Imitate Jesus and Socrates.

A Higher Level

David Copperfield is one of the most successful illusionists of all time. He has a star on the Hollywood Walk of Fame, has won more than twenty Emmy Awards, earned several Guinness World Records, and is consistently listed as one of Forbes top money makers.

On one occasion, David invited my family to his show. We went and we loved it. After the show, David took my son and me to his secret warehouse. David spent hours showing us huge stage props, storage rooms stacked to the ceiling with cases full of illusions, and his collection from past magicians, the largest such collection in the world. David showed us an incredible Houdini collection, including the famous Chinese Water Torture Cell, straightjackets, handcuffs, and even Houdini's baby shoe! While this tour was amazing in many regards, one of the best moments was in the business offices.

We went into a room that had hundreds of video tapes. I was surprised to learn that every single show was videotaped. I asked why, and was told that they wanted to note every un-choreographed moment, both good and bad. They labeled the good moments with a green dot, and any bad moments with a red dot. The "green dot" videos provided David with an invaluable source of great material for future shows, while the "red dot" material was reviewed to eliminate problems from reoccurring.

The process works. When I was in Las Vegas where the show was playing, I noted dozens of billboards for many performers; however, I didn't see many for David Copperfield. David's producer told me that David's show is so stellar, that they simply do not have to advertise as much, and that the theater is always full.

This provided a glimpse into the super achiever mind-set. Achievers have an operational mind-set that shows a high degree of respect for their time. Having had the privilege of spending time with many high achievers, here are some of my observations:

The Future. The achiever knows that all of life will be spent in the future. They know that action is a requirement, or they will spend their lives simply reacting. Achievers learn from the past, but their eyes are on the future.

Time is Life. Most people would never consider self-destruction or suicide, yet some throw away their lives in many wasted minutes and hours. For achievers, time is considered a precious commodity that is jealously guarded. It is thought of in terms of minutes and hours rather than in terms of days, weeks, or months.

Crave a Challenge. Achievers avoid boredom. They crave a challenge, as they know boredom leads to stress and ineffective lives.

Pause and Plan. Days simply go better when a few minutes are spent planning them out.

Identify the Priority. The hallmark of achievement is to focus and handle the top priority. With no priorities, a person or organization becomes a closed system where there is a flurry of activity but nothing is done with any real benefit.

Focus. Achievers aim at the big prize, and let the small ones go to others. There is never time to do everything. Success is a matter of setting priorities and focusing on them. Achievers have a clear focus on what they have to do versus what they want to do. They have a single-minded, focused concentration on the key goal. They never major in minors or spend time on the easy, quick, ineffective activities.

Discipline. Achievers make a habit of doing things that the non-achiever will not do.

Delineate. Creative and administrative tasks are incompatible. They need to be delineated into different parts of the day.

Quality. Achievers know the old saying, "There is never enough time to do it right, but always enough time to do it over." Try to do things right the first time.

Lists. Achievers are chronic "list makers" and never feel too busy to make a list. Focused, successful, effective efforts require a list.

Meetings. An achiever is always considerate of others and will have a clear, written agenda for every meeting. Of course, they will keep the discussion on track and dismiss the meeting on time.

Chapter 20

Consequential

Make History

Leaving Behind a Legacy

When I was a teenager, my dad gave me some advice I'll never forget. He said that whenever I was faced with a big decision, I should think ahead five or ten years and then ask myself if I would look back and be proud of that decision or not. That was good advice. Whether one likes it or not, everyone ultimately owns his or her past activities. Everyone every day is building a legacy.

I have studied my family's legacy. The Bells come from the large Bell clan of Scotland. Some of the family moved from Scotland and my seventh great-grandfather was born in 1627 in York, England. His son, Shadrack Bell, immigrated to New Hampshire soon after the Mayflower landed. His son Thomas colonized in North Carolina. His son Robert was a lieutenant in the Revolutionary War, and his son, William, my third great-grandfather, fought in the Revolutionary War as a private and later established a large plantation in Tennessee that still stands to this day. William's son Alfred moved to Illinois, and later was an early pioneer and moved west. His son, Eli, my great-grandfather, lived in Hawaii and supervised the building of the first sugar mill there. His son, my grandfather Milton Oliver, was very industrious and built and owned seven homes in California. The Depression meant that his

> **Rich Habit #43**
> **Build a Legacy**
>
> Those who maintain a history of their ancestors are up to three times more likely to be happy.

renters lost their jobs, so he lost three of his homes, but he kept going. My dad graduated from UCLA and later headed up research and development at Fender Guitars. He and my mom have spent a total of four and a half years of their lives living with and helping the underprivileged in Mexico, Ecuador, and Peru.

That's the Bells. My other third great-grandfather, John M. Bernhisel, was a doctor from New York who later served five terms in the U.S. Congress. He met regularly with Presidents Fillmore, Pierce, and Lincoln. To top this legacy off, my uncle directed many Hollywood movies and later was a director of *Gilligan's Island,* clearly the benchmark for which all other entertainment is measured!

A good way to honor our ancestors is to remember them and talk about them, while the best way is to try and build upon what they have done. I have read the histories and journals of many of my ancestors, and it strikes me that none of them thought that they were doing much

Prosperity Cycle

The Prosperity Cycle illustrates the common cycle of prosperity, which can lead to arrogance then to disaster and, finally, recovery. Often, this cycle repeats until dysfunction sets in.

This cycle can be broken by integrating *teachable* in the prosperity phase. By continual openness to education, learning, and change, we avoid the pitfalls of arrogance and the disasters it produces.

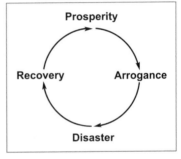

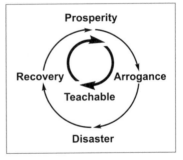

of anything remarkable. In their minds, they were just taking the challenges as they came along and doing their best.

Not everyone has a family legacy to be proud of. I have spent time with teenagers who have flunked out of foster care and who had horrific childhoods. I tell them that they have a unique opportunity to be the one to turn away from the dark past and toward a bright future. They can learn just as much from a bad example as a good example. They can literally change history and put their lives on an upward path. I cannot think of a more impressive legacy than this.

Post-Traumatic Thriving

One time I met a woman named Erica Leon, a Holocaust survivor. Erica told me how she and her family had been devastated. The stories were horrific, yet Erica was so bright and cheerful. She took up art and painted beautiful pictures of her old home in Budapest in bright, striking colors. Her memories were bright, her outlook was brighter. It was fun hanging out with Erica.

I asked Erica a direct question. I asked how she painted such bright pictures of a place that had brought so much pain. I wanted to know why she was so optimistic when she had been dealt such a harsh hand. She said that this was her choice. She made positive thinking her habit. She felt that the clouds in her life had given contrast that allowed her to appreciate the light. She deliberately focused on the light. Erica's life is an example of post-traumatic thriving. Some, like Erica, have gone through a tragedy and have developed a deep sense of resiliency.

I have also spent innumerable hours with people who have gone through the harshest disasters and calamities—re-settlers in Chernobyl, victims of Hurricane Katrina, survivors of the World Trade Center terrorist attacks, and parents who had their homes showered with radioactive fallout from the nuclear tests on Bikini Atoll. They had gone through bitter situations, yet they came out sweet. They had attributes that had apparently lain dormant for decades. While the victims were once everyday people, tragedy awakened them out of their complacency. They emerged far better off than they had been before.

Not everyone navigates successfully out of a crisis, and we can see the measure of a person when he or she is down. Indeed, some solutions are worse than the problem itself. Drugs and alcohol are the most common.

Nothing that is always being stomped and trampled can grow. If we find ourselves in a toxic place, we need to get out of it and seek healthy solutions. Erica and the others did this by simply making the choice.

World Trade Center

The world will never forget September 11, 2001.

I was at home preparing to leave for my office when the phone rang. My wife was taking our daughter and her friend to kindergarten, and her friend's parents had heard the news. My wife called and told me that terrorists had hijacked and crashed planes into the World Trade Center and the Pentagon, another jet had crashed in Pennsylvania, and that the entire World Trade Center had collapsed!

All of the plans for the day were immediately forgotten.

I turned on the television and saw the unthinkable play and replay. Throughout the entire civilized world, everyday life came to an abrupt standstill. My home phone rang, and it was a reporter from the *London Times* who wanted my comments, but I could barely speak.

This was a horrific act with ramifications like no other. Like most businesspeople, I thought, "That could have been me." I flew on American Airlines through Newark all the time. On trips to New York, I would often go to the observation decks at the World Trade Center.

On a practical level, I had an immediate choice to make. I had speaking and business engagements in New York in just a few days. I had to decide whether to go or cancel my trip. My initial inclination was to cancel everything. After two days, I called my airline, and to my surprise, my flights were still scheduled. My clients told me that coming would help people get back into life and move ahead. Still completely overwhelmed, I flew out to New York about a week later. There were only two other passengers on the plane. As my plane made its final approach to Newark Airport, we flew parallel to Manhattan Island. I could see floodlights around the disaster area and the smoke still billowing out. It was a sickening sight.

After my lecture, I took the subway down to ground zero. Although I had seen plenty of pictures in the media, nothing could have prepared me for the disaster in front of me. Skeletons of the lower World Trade Center buildings still leaned askew, and piles of rubble loomed in such a huge, vast area that words and photos couldn't possibly describe the scene. The most haunting memories were the flyers taped everywhere of families looking for loved ones. The smoke was still surging from the rubble. In fact, as I stood there, a manhole I was standing on erupted in flames.

As I ran, the smoke engulfed me and the emergency workers nearby. Later I walked by the fire stations of the lost fire fighters, and was haunted by the numerous hand-made posters with photos of missing loved ones plastered everywhere. Like any disaster, it exposed the true character of those it affected. It not only made an impact on the United States, but it affected the entire freedom-loving world.

Later, the city and state of New York retained me to compute the economic damages to the World Trade Center site. While there has been a great deal spoken about this horrible tragedy—and indeed the damage is unimaginable—there was more to be grateful for. Indeed, gratitude is a habit that is applicable in even the worst of circumstances.

Consider that the World Trade Center was not just the two towers, but also a complex of seven buildings where more than 50,000 people worked and 110,000 people visited on a typical business day. Yet that morning, a two-car accident in the Holland Tunnel blocked traffic and prevented thousands from getting to work on time at the World Trade Center. While, sadly, more than 3,000 people lost their lives, at least 45,000 successfully escaped, were rescued, or were late to work because of the traffic.

In the aftermath of this horrible tragedy, there are many things to be grateful for. Out of more than 100,000 people who were directly targeted by the terrorists, more than 97 percent escaped, survived, or otherwise avoided the attacks.

Today, the Freedom Tower stands on the former World Trade Center site and commands the Manhattan skyline. This 1,776-foot tall structure is a stunning reminder that peaceful people will triumph over terrorism and good over evil. In the aftermath of any tragedy, one can thrive, dive, or merely survive. To me, this Tower signifies post-traumatic thriving.

O. J. Simpson

The O. J. Simpson case captured the attention of the world for more than a year and was labeled by some as the "crime of the century." In June 1994, police found the bodies of Nicole Brown Simpson and her friend Ron Goldman on a walkway leading to Nicole's West Los Angeles condominium. Nicole was the former wife of football legend O. J. Simpson, who lived in a mansion just a few miles from the condominium.

When police arrived at Simpson's mansion, suspicions immediately rose. There was a long history of spousal abuse and Simpson himself had flown to Chicago the night of the murder. A bloody glove was left at the crime scene matching one found at Simpson's estate.

Later it was shown that the victims' blood was in his white Ford Bronco and the blood on the gloves matched both the victims. Simpson had sustained an injury on his hand, and his blood was found at the crime scene. A trail of blood led up Simpson's driveway and into his house. Simpson's houseguest, Brian "Kato" Kaelin, had heard someone walking along the side of the house, exactly where the matching glove had been found. Footprints at the crime scene matched Simpson's foot size.

Even more bizarre, when Simpson's arrest was imminent, he left a rambling note and took cash, his passport, and a disguise and fled the area. He was later found, and the entire city of Los Angeles nearly shut down to watch a strange, low-speed chase as Simpson's friend drove him back to the Rockingham estate.

With few places to go with the evidence, the "Dream Team" defense shifted the focus to Mark Fuhrman, who was portrayed as a racist. Fuhrman actually testified that he had never addressed anyone with a racist term, but again the prosecution never pointed out this distinction and did nothing to defend or rehabilitate him as a witness.

Judge Ito lost control of the courtroom. After a one-and-a-half year trial, and in a highly controversial verdict, Simpson was found not guilty. Later, in another more honorable courtroom, Simpson was subsequently found to be responsible for the deaths and ordered to pay $33.5 million in compensation to Nicole's children and the Goldman families. Simpson also lost his estate located on Rockingham Drive in Brentwood and later went to prison in Nevada on other charges.

I had been involved in measuring the economic impact that the crime stigma had on the Bundy crime scene. Until then, my experiences were largely the same as that of the rest of the world. Then I went through Nicole's condominium and saw the things I had heard about in the news. Nicole's candles were still by the bathtub. I saw the ring left by her ice cream cup on a ledge by the garage. I stood on the spot on the front patio where police believe Simpson hid and spied through the window. I walked the walkway itself where the murders occurred. I stood by the tree stump where Ron Goldman's body was found.

On one occasion, I went by the office of Lou Brown, Nicole's father, to drop off some paperwork. I had my daughter with me who, at the time, was a year old. My intention was to simply drop off the package at the reception area. Lou happened to be there, and he asked me to stay a few minutes. Lou Brown was a great guy, a very kind man and a grandfatherly figure. He had no interest in talking to me—he wanted to talk to and hold my beautiful little daughter. As Lou held her, I was jolted into a sobering perspective of this whole event. He was holding my little girl, but he had lost his. At that moment, the event went from a media circus to a horrible tragedy.

Losing a daughter or sister under such circumstances must have been an unbearable experience for the Brown family. The jury verdict in the criminal trial added to this devastation.

Many people would have been irreparably crushed by this experience. Remarkably, the Browns channeled their anger, grief, and frustration into a positive effort to help battered women. Denise and other members of the family have used the media attention from this event to increase the public's awareness of spousal abuse. As a result, many abused women have been helped during a time that might otherwise have seemed hopeless.

The Brown family shared with me that they were simply in the daily habit of showing love and support to each other. They forgave quickly and easily. They simply made a choice to honor their daughter's and sister's memory by continuing in that support, and to extend it to others.

Denise Brown's work of educating people about domestic violence is a textbook example of post-traumatic thriving. I have been to many events where women have told me that they are alive because of Denise's efforts. That is a remarkable legacy.

Jimmy Bags

I work with some incredible people. One day I was having lunch with Jim Kearns, one of my colleagues. Jim was telling me that he wanted to help the homeless, but that he was reluctant to give them money.

Still wanting to do something, his solution was to get some plastic bags and put in bottles of water, some snack bars along with some basic items. He carries them in his car and gives them out when he sees a homeless person who is asking for something.

I loved this idea, and my youngest son and I spent part of a weekend putting together similar bags. I also put in some information on resources for the homeless, so that if they are sincere about getting back on their feet, they will know where to go. In my colleague's honor, we call them "Jimmy Bags." Then we started handing out Jimmy Bags ourselves.

Since then, I have told others about this. One friend of mine who lives in Melbourne, Australia, loved the idea and he now hands out Jimmy Bags. Another friend from England now does the same. Nobody knows just how far Jim's legacy will go.

Small things can make a huge difference. Jim had no agenda to start any kind of movement—he only wanted to do the right thing and happened to mention it to me. But the right thing got noticed and now homeless people in both hemispheres are a little better off. We are all in a position to do something. We can solve a problem and share the solution.

Better Than We Found It

One of our family mottos is, "Leave things better than we found them." We see examples of this with Denise Brown's efforts to educate, Erica Leon's artwork, the Freedom Tower built out of the World Trade Center ashes, and Jimmy Bags.

For the rest of us, this can take many forms, from cheering up a store clerk or a fellow worker who is not having his or her best day, to raising children who are happy and productive, to spending years with a business to help it run more productively. If we approach each situation with the attitude that we are going to leave it better than we found it, we will inherently create a great legacy.

Building a legacy also demands that we understand that life is a test. We must start where we are and then build on that. To ultimately pass this test, we must appreciate and enjoy all of the good things, while also knowing that hurdles are going to be thrown our way. Those who are genuinely successful know that it is inevitable—problems are a part of every life and every organization's landscape. Nobody has ever built a great legacy by avoiding problems. Anyone who has built a noteworthy legacy did so by facing challenges and overcoming them.

Organizations must maneuver and work to remain viable in a world that is increasingly cluttered and competing for attention. Businesses will have to meet the challenges of competition and continuous research and training.

Parents face the challenges of raising good children in a world full of risk, keeping impossible schedules, continually teaching, paying all the endless costs to keeping a household running and, while doing all of this, putting in quality time together as a family.

Achievement takes work. There is no honor for the timid or those who have had everything handed to them. No one can build a legacy by avoiding and circumventing problems. There is no greatness in just doing the same old thing the way it has always been done. To build a genuine legacy, we must improve upon the status quo, take the challenges, and then conquer them. The harder the test, the greater the joy in passing it.

A positive attitude does not mean we get suckered into the self-absorbed and delusional notions that we think we're important because some success guru says we are, or doing jumping jacks while chanting that we can do anything. A positive attitude is grounded in the reality that we must take full responsibility for our lives and decisions, being grateful for what we have, and taking the steps to reach even higher levels.

One of history's greatest books, *Man's Search for Meaning,* was not written by a king, president, or top CEO. It was written by a Jewish prisoner who spent three years in Nazi concentration camps. Viktor Frankl beat the 1:29 odds of survival and had this to say about it: "Man is ultimately self-determining. What he becomes—within reason of endowment and environment—he has made out of himself. In the concentration camps, for example, in this living laboratory and this testing ground, we watched and witnessed some of our comrades behave like swine while others behaved like saints. Man has both potentialities within himself; which one is actualized depends on decisions but not on conditions."[126]

Chapter 21

Consequential

The Next Step for *Be*

The Art of Life

One of the attributes of the four cornerstones is that even the youngest children can understand *Me We Do Be*. Yet, these same four cornerstones have been the foundation in many boardroom discussions where millions of dollars are at stake.

Me is where we build knowledge and wisdom. We think, do our homework, and focus upon our thoughts, feelings, and attitudes. The *Me* habits mean that we don't just live day-to-day and react to whatever is thrown at us, but that we study and carefully choose our direction. Here we spend time in deep thought to develop intellectually, spiritually, and philosophically. We think, study, meditate, pray, and ponder. We take time to turn off all the noise, knowing that great insights already reside inside of us if we only take the time to listen.

Rich Habit #44 Make It Happen!	
Of all *Be* habits, procrastination is ranked as the number one worst.	
Worst Be Habits	
Habit	**Index**
Procrastination	250
Not being on time	119
Being lazy	57

For students, this could mean reflecting on their areas of study and selecting a major that is right for them. For businesspeople, this could mean taking some quiet time at the start of every day to reflect on the mission of the company and to plan their day. For a parent, this could mean thinking about each member of the family and how to best care for each one. The result of our life experience is that we become like what we worship.

In the concept of *We* is where we build relationships. Here we connect with the right people and build our circle of success. With this cornerstone, we develop culturally, sociologically, and influentially. We build social capital and avoid toxic people. Here we recognize that the most powerful force on the earth is kindness.

For a student, this could mean connecting with the right professors and the right groups, teams, and clubs. For a businessperson, this could mean showing appreciation to staff, vendors, and customers who make the business run. For a parent, this could mean giving clear responsibilities to each family member, supporting the dreams of each one, and just spending time having fun.

Do is where we build our productivity. Here we examine our level of utility and productivity. Here is the declaration that "I will serve" or "I will be productive" financially, physically, and environmentally.

For a student, this could mean working hard on school projects, living within a budget, and keeping fit. For a businessperson, *Do* could mean adding value to the company, customers, and clients and producing quality products and services. For a parent, this could mean keeping spending within the family budget, keeping the home tidy, the chores organized, serving healthy meals, and building family traditions. For everyone, the *Do* habits are a commitment to produce something and create value.

Be is where we build the future. Here we develop and set goals, manage our time, and document our achievements. Ultimately, with this cornerstone, we contribute to building something bigger than ourselves. Here we break out of our comfort zones, set goals, and use our time to create something timeless.

For a student, this could mean improving his or her report cards and keeping a journal. For a businessperson, this could mean setting goals, managing time wisely, and adding to his or her resume. For a parent, this could mean setting family goals, and keeping family photos, videos, and journals of the journey. Combined, the *Me We Do Be* cornerstones lay a solid foundation. They insure that we are grounded and on solid footing in life, business, and with our families and friends.

History's Lessons

Benjamin Franklin said, "Either write something worth reading or do something worth writing." We might all carry two books: one to read, and one to write in. A life worth living is a life worth recording. Diaries and journals share our lessons, as well as how we lived and enjoyed the journey. Plus, the journals of our seemingly unremarkable lives, both the triumphs and the tragedies, will be of remarkable value going forward.

History is today viewed a hundred years from now. When we have a legacy mind-set and place something into our own time capsules, we perpetuate the timeless progression of mankind.

All of history's great achievers applied *Be* habits. They set goals, managed their time, and documented their journey. Thomas Edison, who invented the light bulb, started a pocket notebook in October 1870. He stated, "All new inventions I will hereafter keep a full record." From this point on he did, which resulted in more than a dozen technical notebooks, many of which contain beautiful drawings.

Alexander Graham Bell's papers included diaries, correspondence, printed matter, financial and legal records, and several hundred volumes of laboratory notebooks that recorded his daily work from 1865 to 1922. These have been invaluable in the fields of aeronautics, eugenics, and physics.

> ### Rich Habit #45
> ### Teach
>
> When asked about their greatest accomplishments, a predictable trio of family, education, and health emerged.
>
> However, teaching was the only vocation that made the list. Even if your profession is not as a teacher, helping and teaching others is richly satisfying.

Christopher Columbus said, "I determined to keep an account of the voyage, and to write down punctually everything we performed or saw from day to day, as will hereafter appear. I intend to draw up a nautical chart, which shall contain the several parts of the ocean and land in their proper situations; and also to compose a book to represent the whole by pictures with latitudes and longitudes, on all which accounts it behooves me to abstain from my sleep, and make many trials in navigation, which things will demand much labor."

The key reason we know so much about Benjamin Franklin is that he wrote volumes about what he thought and how he lived, including journals, essays, books, newspaper articles, ballads, almanacs, letters, and an autobiography. Sir Ernest Shackleton's Endurance Diary and other journals are also prized possessions.

Spiritual, philosophical, and religious figures have also implemented these principles. Moses preserved the Ten Commandments that had been carved in stone. He also documented the story of the Israelites' deliverance from bondage in Egypt. Jesus clearly was a strong student of historical writings and often began a teaching with the statement, "It is written . . ." He told his followers to spread his message.

Buddha had his followers record his teachings and frequently said that even death is not to be feared by one who has lived wisely. Muhammad taught, "Conduct yourself in this world as if you are here to stay forever, and yet prepare for eternity as if you are to die tomorrow."

Plato, a student of Socrates and teacher of Aristotle, documented his legacy in many writings including his most famous work, *The Republic*. Aristotle, who developed the scientific method and the concept of empirical research, meticulously wrote about his work in formal logic, zoology, metaphysics, and geology.

We all have insights, experiences, and thoughts that are unique to us. The *Be* habits include documenting our journey and preserving our lessons.

A Book to Write In

When I was in high school, I was at the home of a friend whose father was a well-known author. I asked him how he was able to write so many books, and I'll never forget his response. He said that he just got up about forty-five minutes earlier than his family and wrote a page or two a day. That all added up to a new book every year!

I adopted a version of this habit. Late at night or when sitting on a plane, I write down my experiences, observations, and lessons in a journal. I always carry my black journal with me.

My first cornerstone Me habit is to always carry an inspirational book to read, but my *Be* cornerstone is to carry around a book to write in. Documenting my life's journey is my cornerstone *Be* habit.

Wealth Has Its Limits

I once had some business dealings with a Hollywood producer. He had produced many major films and had been the president of a major Hollywood studio for years. Once we met at his office on the studio lot, and his walls were covered with photographs of himself with every imaginable movie star and political figure. His office was full of mementos that had been given to him by all kinds of famous people.

We then went to his house in Beverly Hills and sat in his private movie viewing room. Again, we were surrounded by mementos of his success. We had dinner served by his butler, and the two of us walked around his grounds and tennis court. He told me about his two famous and beautiful ex-wives. He took me over to a tree where a friend of his—a famous musician—had gotten married. We walked over to the tennis court, and he showed me the umpire chair given to him by a famous movie star.

Soon the conversation took a personal turn, and he told me about how he'd had nothing when he was young and about major risks he had taken along the road to success. He started to cry when he told me about his divorce from one of his famous wives, and that he had been at fault for putting movie projects ahead of her. He then told me something I will never forget.

"Randall," he said, *"do you know what has motivated me to achieve all of this? When you're dead, you're dead, but my name appears at the front of dozens of famous movies, and in that way, I will always be alive!"*

To me, this is a pretty sad view of immortality. Fame is fleeting. My philosophy about money and success is quite different. Money is great—even essential—but it is not life. Like air, money is a vital component for life, but it should be kept in perspective. Genuine legacies don't have much to do with fame or money.

The Butterfly Effect

Whenever one of my children goes off to a dance, I give him or her the same advice my mom gave to me when I was a teenager. She told me to be sure to ask some girls to dance who hadn't yet been asked. She told me that tiny things could change the trajectory of a person's life. I didn't know a "trajectory" was, but I did what she asked.

The Butterfly Effect is a term coined by mathematician Edward Lorenz to describe how a small change in one place can set off a chain of events that has a large effect somewhere else. The Butterfly Effect demonstrates that the tiny amount of air stirred up by a butterfly's wings can actually set off a series of events that can change the weather patterns on the other side of the world. Likewise, just a tiny drop of rain in Palau or Saipan can start a chain reaction that creates a wave in Laguna Beach.

In a world full of fast, loud, thundering messages, tiny things still matter. Both sailors and pilots agree that an error of just one degree will mean missing their destination by hundreds of miles. In sports, milliseconds, millimeters, or the tiniest angle of a tennis racket or golf club can mean defeat or victory.

> **Rich Habit #46**
> **Dancing**
> 73.5 percent of those people who dance are happy.

Life offers time and freedom. In a society where the average person is assaulted with hundreds of distractions a day, the *Be* habits are small and are simple concepts that can be built upon with just moments a day. We are the sum of tiny thoughts and habits.

The Butterfly Effect teaches that tiny things matter, and there is no such thing as a tiny drop in the bucket. Our daily, tiny choices truly matter. These efforts all add up to a powerful life with purpose and can have an influence that can be felt around the world.

More than thirty years after my last high-school dance, I was at a dinner party where one of other guests was a women I had gone to high school with. She took me aside and started to cry. She told me that she had once gone to a dance feeling very nervous about some deep personal problems. She thanked me, thirty years later, for simply coming up to her and saying, "Hi," and asking her to dance. It not only changed her entire outlook for the rest of the dance, but it helped her change her outlook of a bleak situation.

I simply had no idea. I was simply doing something that my mom told me. But this was a profound moment when I realized that my mom was right. I went home and finally got a dictionary and looked up the word, "trajectory."

Using Time to Create the Timeless

The solutions to many problems are yet to be discovered. There are great pursuits yet to be accomplished in art, science, athletics, politics, business, philosophy, religion, technology, medicine, parenting, and more.

While there are many great pursuits, they will all be built by those who have the same fundamental foundation. All of history's great achievers—from Einstein, Churchill, Lincoln, to Aristotle—complied with certain universal laws. Future achievers will do the same.

Do not underestimate the importance of our daily habits. In my consulting work, I have worked on major disaster sites throughout the world. When something goes wrong, it can usually be traced to a crack in one of the *Me We Do Be* principles. Chernobyl happened because of cracks in the first cornerstone. Some scientists who lacked the intelligence and core values to follow set safety guidelines conducted an unauthorized test that led to the world's worst nuclear disaster. The Titanic sank because ego was put in front of safety. The World Trade Center attack happened because hatred overrode everything else.

But there are good examples as well. Denise Brown, a sister of Nicole Brown Simpson, set a goal to help women who are in toxic relationships. Erica Leon overcame the holocaust and now paints stunning pictures. Everyone survived the Durham Woods pipeline explosion because the community was full of good neighbors.

The more things change, the more they stay the same. These principles are universal laws. There are few things that great academics, philosophers, CEOs, presidents, prophets, and social scientists all seem to agree on. Yet they all solidly agree on building upon the habits, rituals, and routines that can be summed up as *Me We Do Be*.

There is a distinct segment of the population that has intentionally chosen to live within what I call an "elevated realm." Reflective thinking, kind acts, and authentic ethics dominate their daily rituals. They shun counterfeit highs and thrills almost as much as they are repelled by self-righteousness. They have discovered that a "helper's high" is far more satisfying than accumulating more stuff. They clearly distinguish between need and greed and know that money has an important but limited role in a rich life.

The cumulative science and statistical evidence is clear: the greatest joy comes from an illuminated mind-set, kind and generous relationships with family and close friends, and making continual progress. Those in the elevated realm do not frantically chase money, social status, or an inflated image, but they naturally attract a balanced level of prosperity. They function best in a clean and organized environment and they treasure their health and their time. They play, laugh a lot, and count their blessings. They honor the legacy of those who came before, and they do something to contribute and build upon what they have been given.

You were born an original, so don't die as a copy of what others want you to be. Make your mark. From my work with the world's biggest crises to volunteering with homeless shelters and at-risk teenagers, I see that just one bad habit can spread out until it overwhelms everything. The great secret is that the opposite is just as true: one new good habit will ripple out until it entirely engulfs a life or an organization. If you are not in the elevated realm you want, start by choosing just one new *Me We Do Be* habit. Make it simple and easy. Then do it honestly and repeatedly. It will take root and gradually grow until you are in an entirely new sphere.

The *Be* Challenge Coin

This is where you accept the challenge coin and take responsibility for your own *Be* cornerstone. This is where you do something to build the future; specifically, pick a target, make it happen, and make history.

Avoid the January 4th effect. Pick only one new *Be* habit and make it simple. For example, don't commit to writing in your journal for thirty minutes a day; rather, commit to spending one minute, but more if you choose to. Commit to mastering your new *Be* habit and make it a solid cornerstone of your life. Here are some suggestions, or come up with one of your own:

- Write down your top goals in life.
- Post your list of goals and review them daily.
- Find out what your passion is and contribute to that community.
- Spend _____ number of hours per week working toward your goals.
- Keep a calendar.
- Spend_____number of minutes planning out your day.
- Maintain a To Do list.
- Maintain a To Not Do list.
- Be _____ number of minutes early to every appointment.
- Create art.
- Write a book.
- Learn to dance.
- Teach a class.
- Write in a journal every_____ amount of time.
- Learn to play a new musical instrument.
- Get a new hobby.
- Set up a chore schedule for your children.
- Collect and maintain your family's history.
- Organize your family photos.
- Spend_____hours every week teaching your children
- Teach a class on _____ number of skills you have learned.

Four Cornerstones

	Concepts	Categories	Applications
Me	FIAT LUX *Let There Be Light* Habits That Build Wisdom	Intellectual Philosophical Spiritual	Think Believe Feel
We	EX CARITAS *Out of Kindness, Love & Gratitude* Habits That Build Relationships	Sociological Influential Cultural	Teamwork Communication Style
Do	SERVIUM *I Will Produce* Habits That Build Productivity	Physical Financial Environmental	Fitness Budget Space
Be	AB AETERNO *Of The Eternities* Habits That Build The Future	Developmental Operational Consequential	Goals Time Mgt Legacy

Thriving Behaviors		Toxic Behaviors	
ILLUMINATION	Continually Learn	Know It All	DISTRACTION
	Stand for Something	Fall for Anything	
	Connect with a Higher Power	Slip Into Spiritual Poverty	
CONNECTION	Elevate Your Team	Deflate Your Team	ALIENATION
	Express Yourself	Don't Communicate	
	Spice It Up!	Blend In	
PRODUCTION	Keep In Shape	Neglect Your Health	STAGNATION
	Add Value	Get Into Debt	
	Enjoy Your View	Accumulate Clutter	
PROGRESSION	Pick a Target	Wander Aimlessly	DESTRUCTION
	Make It Happen	Wonder What Happened	
	Make History	Just Get By	

Four Cornerstones

The four cornerstones of a fulfilling life are:

Me-something to believe,

We-someone to love,

Do-something to do, and

Be-someone to become.

Habits, Rituals, & Routines

Note how some habits might fit into morning and evening rituals. Avoid the mistake of adopting too many new habits. It is overwhelming. Instead, pick one or two new habits. They will naturally grow.

Rich Habits	Poor Habits
Morning Ritual	**Morning Ritual**
• Wake up early	• Wake up late
• Exercise	• Rush out the door
• Read	• Grab processed or fast food
• Meditate, pray	
• Plan out day	
Daily Habits	**Daily Habits**
• Play audio books	• Listen to radio while driving
• Build social capital	• Gossip
• Save and invest	• Watch the clock
• Count calories	• Borrow on credit card
• Be punctual	• Fast food lunch
• Document insights	
• Get the job done	
Evening Ritual	**Evening Ritual**
• Dinner as a family	• Watch too much of television
Weekly Routines	**Weekly Routines**
• Call family & friends	• Loaf around
• Volunteer	• Watch a lot of television and Internet
• Worship service	
• Send thank you cards	
• Do something fun	

Bibliography & Recommended Reading

Habits and Thinking Strategy

Duhigg, Charles. The Power of Habit: Why we do what we do in Life and Business. Random House LLC, 2012.

Collins, James Charles. Good To Great: Why Some Companies Make the Leap . . . And Others Don't. Random House, 2001.

Covey, Stephen. The Seven Habits of Highly Successful People.

Arbinger Institute, The. Leadership and Self Deception: Getting Out of the Box, 2002.

The Me Cornerstone

Ferrucci, Piero. The Power of Kindness: The Unexpected Benefits of Leading a Compassionate Life. Penguin, 2007.

Lyubomirsky, Sonja. The How of Happiness: A Scientific Approach to Getting the Life You Want. Penguin, 2008.

Peale, Norman Vincent. The Power of Positive Thinking. Random House, 2012.

Warren, Richard. The Purpose-driven Life: What on Earth Am I Here For? Zondervan, 2002.

The We Cornerstone

Carnegie, Dale. How to Win Friends and Influence People. Inktree, 1938.

Johnson, Spencer, and Kenneth Blanchard. The One-Minute Manager. Video Publishing House, 1986.

Johnson, Spencer. Who Moved my Cheese?: An Amazing Way to Deal with Change in your Work and in your Life. Random House, 1999.

Mandino, Og. The Greatest Miracle in the World. Random House LLC, 1975.

The Do Cornerstone

Clason, George S. The Richest Man in Babylon. Giuseppe Castrovilli, 1955.

Hill, Napoleon. Think and Grow Rich. Dutton Adult, 1972. Kiyosaki, Robert T. and Sharon L. Lechter. Rich Dad, Poor Dad. Grand Central, 1998.

The Be Cornerstone

Coelho, Paulo. The Alchemist. Harper Collins, 2007.

Frankl, Viktor. Man's Search for Meaning. Simon and Schuster, 1985.

Pausch, Randy, and Jeffrey Zaslow. The Last Lecture. Hachette UK, 2010.

Tracy, Brian. Eat that Frog!: 21 Great Ways to Stop Procrastinating and Get More Done in Less Time. Berrett-Koehler Publishers, 2007.

Endnotes

[1]Ann Graybiel, "Overview at Habits, Rituals, and the Evaluative Brain," Annual Review of Neuroscience 31 (2008): 359–87.

[2]Affluenza: How to be Successful and Stay Sane. London: Vermilion. p. 344. ISBN 978-0-09-190010-6.

[3]Affluenza: The All-Consuming Epidemic, John de Graaf, David Wann, & Thomas H. Naylor, ISBN 1-57675-199-6.

[4]Charles Duhigg, The Power of Habit: Why We Do What We Do In Life and Business. (New York: Random House, 2012).

[5] David T. Neal, Wendy Wood, and Jeffery M. Quinn, "Habits—A Repeat Performance," Current Direction in Psychological Science 15, no. 4 (2006): 198–202. See also, Henk Aarts, Theo Paulussen, and Herman Schaalma, "Physical Exercise Habit: On the Capitalization and Formation of Habitual Health Behaviors," Health Education Research 12 (1997): 363–74.

[6] Alain Dagher and T. W. Robbins, "Personality, Addiction, Dopamine: Insights from Parkinson's Disease," Neuron 61 (2009): 502–10.

[7]Duhigg, op. cit.

[8]Karl Weick, "Small Wins: Redefining the Scale of Social Problems," American Psychologist 39 (1984): 40–49.

[9]Duhigg, op cit. See also, Kent C. Berridge and Morten L. Kringelbach, "Affective Neuroscience of Pleasure: Reward in Humans and Animals," Psychopharmacology 199 (2008): 457–80. See also, Wolfram Schutz, "Behavioral Theories and the Neurophysiology of Reward," Annual Review of Psychology 57 (2006): 87–115.

[10]Ron Suskind, The Price of Loyalty: George W. Bush, the White House, and the Education of Paul O'Neill. (New York: Simon & Schuster Paperbacks, 2004). See also, Michael Lewis, "O'Neill's List," New York Times, January 13, 2002.

[11]Duhigg, op. cit.

[12]This homeless shelter is focused on adults who are actively seeking employment. In 2012, the Friendship Shelter had a 68 percent success rate and the Henderson House had a 92 percent success rate. "About US," Friendship Shelter, accessed December 16, 2014, http://friendshipshelter.org/welcome.php.

[13]The name Danny is a pseudonym.

[14]Todd F. Heatherton and Patricia A. Nichols, "Personal Accounts of Successful Versus Failed Attempts at Life Change," Personality and Social Psychology Bulletin 20, no. 6 (1994): 664–75.

[15] Bill O'Hanlon, Do One Thing Different. (New York: HarperCollins, 1999). See also, Karl Weick, "Small Wins: Redefining the Scale of Social Problems," American Psychologist 39 (1984): 40–49. See also, S. M. Rebro, et al., "The Effect of Keeping Food Records on Eating Patterns," Journal of the American Diatetic Association 98 (1998): 1163–65.

[16]Dilanthi Amaratunga, David Baldry, and Marjan Sarshar, "Process Improvement through Performance Measurement: The Balanced Scorecard Methodology," Work Study, Vol. 50, Issue: 5 (2001): 179–189.

[17]Benjamin Libet, "Unconscious Cerebral Initiative and the Role of Conscious Will in Voluntary Action," Neurophysiology of Consciousness. (1993): 269–306.

[18]The theme of light and illumination is at the core of both academic and religious institutions. Several universities have a motto centered on "light. For example, the motto for both UCLA and Berkeley is "Let there be light" and Yale is "Lux et Veritas" meaning, "Light and Truth." Columbia University is "In lumine tuo videbimus lumen" meaning "In Thy light shall we see light." The motto of the University of Cambridge is, "Hinc lucem et pocula sacra," meaning, "From here, light and sacred draughts." Oxford has a religious theme of "Dominus Illuminatio mea" meaning, "The Lord is My Light." See also, Genesis 1:3, "And God said, Let there be light, and there was light."

[19]Maxwell Anderson, Joan of Lorraine: A Play in Two Acts. New York: Dramatists Play Service, Inc, 1946.

[20] Some of these situations and insights were previously discussed within my book, Strategy 360. See Randall Bell, Strategy 360. Laguna Beach, CA: Owners Manual Press, 2009.

[21]John Emsley, Uranium." Nature's Building Blocks: An A to Z Guide to the Elements. Oxford: Oxford University Press, 2001, 476–482.

[22]Ken Joweitt, "Soviet Neotraditionalism: The Political Corruption of a Leninist Regime," Soviet Studies 35, no. 3 (1983): 275–297.

[23]Marc Gerstein and Michael Ellsberg, Flirting With Disaster. New York: Sterling Publishing Co., Inc., 2008, 103.

[24]Jean Grugel and Pia Riggirozzi, "Post-neoliberalism in Latin America: Rebuilding and Reclaiming the State after Crisis." Development and Change 43, no. 1 (2012): 1–21.

[25]Philip Brickman, Dan Coates, and Ronnie Janoff-Bulman. "Lottery Winners and Accident Victims: Is Happiness Relative?" Journal of Personality and Social Psychology 36, no. 8 (1978): 917.

[26]Philip Brickman, Dan Coates, and Ronnie Janoff-Bulman. "Lottery Winners and Accident Victims: Is Happiness Relative?" Journal of Personality and Social Psychology 36, no. 8 (1978): 917.

[27]Martin EP Seligman and Mihaly Csikszentmihalyi, "Positive Psychology: An Introduction," American Psychological Association, 55, no. 1, (2000). See also, Sonja Lyubomirsky, The How of Happiness: A Scientific Approach to Getting the Life you Want. (New York: Penguin, 2008).

[28]Lynette L. Craft and Frank M. Perna, "The Benefits of Exercise for the Clinically Depressed," Primary Care Companion to the Journal of Clinical Psychiatry 6, no. 3 (2004): 104.

[29]"Role of Endorphins Discovered." PBS Online: A Science Odyssey: People and Discoveries, accessed January 6, 2014, http://www.pbs.org/wgbh/aso/databank/entries/dh75en.html.

[30] Newton Hightower and David C. Kay. Anger Busting 101: The New ABC's for Angry Men and the Women who Love Them. Houston: Bayou Pub., 2005.

[31]L. Roberts, D. Salem, J. Rappaport, P. A. Toro, D. A. Luke, and E. Seidman (1999). "Giving and Receiving Help: Interpersonal Transactions in Mutual-help Meetings and Psychosocial Adjustment of Members," American Journal of Community Psychology, 27, no. 6 (1987): 841–868.

[32]Daniel M. Wegner, David J. Schneider, Samuel R. Carter, and Teri L. White. "Paradoxical Effects of Thought Suppression." Journal of Personality and Social Psychology, 53, no. 1 (1987): 5.

[33]R. Lippitt, J. Watson, and B. Westley, Dynamics of Planned Change, New York: Harcourt Brace, 1958.

[34]A. Grant and F. Gino, "A Little Thanks Goes a Long Way: Explaining Why Gratitude Expressions Motivate Prosocial Behavior," Journal of Personality and Social Psychology, 98, no. 6 (2010): 946–955.

[35]This concept is attributed to Zig Zigler.

[36]When I consult on a disaster, I have a preset series of steps in mind. W. W. Burke, Organization Development: A Process of Learning and Changing. (Reading, MA: Addison-Wesley, 1993). See also, A. Casey and E. Goldman, "Enhancing the Ability to Think Strategically: A Learning Model," 41, 2 (2010): 167–185. See also, V. Cheng, J. Rhodes, and P. Lok, "A Framework for Strategic Decision Making and Performance among Chinese Managers," The International Journal of Human Resource Management, 21, 9 (2010): 1373–1395. S.R. Covey, The 7 Habits of Highly Effective People: Powerful Lessons in Personal Change. New York, NY: Simon & Schuster, 1989.

[37]H. Levinson, Organizational Diagnosis. Cambridge, MA: Harvard University Press, 1972.

[38]Olivia Bruner, Playstation Nation: Protect your child from video game addiction. Center Street, 2006.

[39]Ibid.

[40]Richard Paul and Linda Elder, Critical Thinking: Learn the Tools the Best Thinkers Use. Pearson/Prentice Hall, 2006.

[41]D. Gopher, L. Armony and Y. Greenspan, "Switching Tasks and Attention Policies," Journal of Experimental Psychology: General, 129, (2000): 308–229.

[42]Barbara B. Gray, "Don't Want to Overeat? Stop Multitasking at Mealtime!" Health (2013).

[43]Guy Winch, Emotional First Aid: Practical Strategies for Treating Failure, Rejection, Guilt, and Other Everyday Psychological Injuries. Exisle Publishing, 2013. See also, D. Gopher, L. Armony, and Y. Greenspan, "Switching Tasks and Attention Policies," Journal of Experimental Psychology: General, 129 (2000): 308–229. See also, U. Mayr and R. Kliegl, "Task-set Switching and Long-term Memory Retrieval." Journal of Experimental Psychology: Learning, Memory, and Cognition, 26, (2000): 1124–1140. See also, S. Monsell, R. Azuma, M. Eimer, M. Le Pelley, and S. Strafford, "Does a prepared task switch require an extra (control) process between stimulus onset and response selection?" (poster presented at the 18th International Symposium on Attention and Performance, Windsor Great Park, United Kingdom, July, 1998). See also, "Phones, Texting May Be as Dangerous as Alcohol for Drivers," Health (2013).

[44]Walter Mischel and Nancy Baker, "Cognitive Appraisals and Transformations in Delay Behavior." Journal of Personality and Social Psychology 31, no. 2 (1975): 254. See also, Yuichi Shoda, Walter Mischel, and Philip K. Peake. "Predicting Adolescent Cognitive and Self-regulatory Competencies from Preschool Delay of Gratification: Identifying Diagnostic Conditions." Developmental Psychology 26, no. 6 (1990): 978.

[45]John Robst, "Education and Job Match: The Relatedness of College Major and Work." Economics of Education Review 26, no. 4 (2007): 397–407.

[46]John F. Carter and Nicholas H. Van Matre, "Note Taking Versus Note Having." Journal of Educational Psychology 67, no. 6 (1975): 900.

[47]William Aiken and Hugh LaFollette. World Hunger and Morality. Ed. 2. Prentice-Hall Inc., 1996.

[48]Herbert Fingarette, Self-Deception: With a New Chapter. Univ. of California Press, 2000. See also, Eduardo Giannetti, Lies We Live By: The Art of Self-deception. Bloomsbury Publishing UK, 2001.

[49]William Strawbridge, Richard Cohen, Sarah Shema, and George Kaplan, "Frequent Attendance at Religious Services and Mortality over 28 Years," American Journal of Public Health 87 (1997): 957–61.

[50]Hendrik Simon Versnel, Faith, Hope and Worship: Aspects of Religious Mentality in the Ancient World. Vol. 2. Brill Archive, 1981.

[51]Daniel Garber, What Happens after Pascal's Wager: Living Faith and Rational Belief. Marquette Univ. Pr., 2009.

[52]Mark Twain, The Complete Works of Mark Twain. Kartindo, 1907.

[53]John M. Darley and C. Daniel Batson. "From Jerusalem to Jericho: A Study of Situational and Dispositional Variables in Helping Behavior." Journal of Personality and Social Psychology 27, no. 1 (1973): 100.

[54]The is paraphrased from the quote attributed to Charles Darwin, "It is not the strongest or the species that survives, nor the most intelligent that survives. It is the one that is most adaptable to change."

[55] Muzafer Sherif, The Robbers Cave Experiment: Intergroup Conflict and Cooperation, orig. pub. as Intergroup Conflict and Group Relations. Wesleyan University Press, 1961. See also, Oliver J. Harvey, B. Jack White, William R. Hood, and Carolyn W. Sherif. Intergroup Conflict and Cooperation: The Robbers Cave Experiment. Vol. 10. Norman, OK: University Book Exchange, 1961.

[56]Alejandro Portes, "Social Capital: Its Origins and Applications in Modern Sociology," LESSER, Eric L. Knowledge and Social Capital. Boston: Butterworth-Heinemann (2000): 43–67.

[57]C. Lewis, Surround Yourself With Greatness. Salt Lake, UT: Shadow Mountain, 2009.

[58]Philip G. Zimbardo, Christina Maslach, and Craig Haney. "Reflections on the Stanford Prison Experiment: Genesis, Transformations, Consequences." Obedience to Authority: Current Perspectives on the Milgram Paradigm (2000): 193–237.

[59]G. Morgan, Images of Organization. Thousand Oaks, CA: Sage Publications, 2006.

[60]Paul Hersey, Kenneth H. Blanchard, and Walter E. Natemeyer. "Situational Leadership, Perception, and the Impact of Power," Group & Organization Management 4, no. 4 (1979): 418–428.

[61]D. J. Hughesand M. T. Burgy. "Reflection of Neutrons from Magnetized Mirrors." Physical Review 81, no. 4 (1951): 498. See also, Vittorio Gallese and Alvin Goldman. "Mirror Neurons and the Simulation Theory of Mind-reading." Trends in Cognitive Sciences 2, no. 12 (1998): 493–501.

[62]Richard E. Nisbett and Timothy D. Wilson. "The Halo Effect: Evidence for Unconscious Alteration of Judgments." Journal of Personality and Social Psychology 35, no. 4 (1977): 250.

[63]Richard M. Emerson "Social Exchange Theory." Annual Review of Sociology (1976): 335–362.

[64]Ibid.

[65]Ibid.

[66]Donald T. Phillips, The Founding Fathers on Leadership: Classic Teamwork in Changing Times. Hachette Digital, Inc., 2001.

[67]Piero Ferrucci, The Power of Kindness: The Unexpected Benefits of Leading a Compassionate Life. New York, NY: Penguin Group, 2006.

[68]Mitchel G. Adler and Nancy S. Fagley. "Appreciation: Individual Differences in Finding Value and Meaning as a Unique Predictor of Subjective Well-Being." Journal of personality 73, no. 1 (2005): 79–114. See also, J. L. Smith, Valued Employees Get Results. Quality, 49, 8 (2010): 14.

[69]Xavier Sala-i-Martin, "The World Distribution of Income: Falling Poverty and . . . Convergence, Period." The Quarterly Journal of Economics (2006): 351–397.

[70]American Psychiatric Association. Diagnostic and Statistical Manual of Mental Disorders. Arlington, VA: American Psychiatric Association, 2000.

[71]Otto Kernberg, "Borderline Personality Organization." Journal of the American Psychoanalytic Association 15, no. 3 (1967): 641–685. See also, Bill Eddy and Randi Kreger, Splitting: Protect Yourself While Divorcing Someone with Borderline or Narcissistic Personality Disorder. California: New Harbinger Publications, 2011.

[72]Martha Stout, The Sociopath Next Door. New York, NY: Broadway Books, 2005.

[73]Eddy and Kreger, op cit.

[74]Solomon E. Asch, "Effects of Group Pressure upon the Modification and Distortion of Judgments." Groups, Leadership, and Men (1951): 222–236.

[75]Sheldene Simola, "Ethics of Justice and Care in Corporate Crisis Management." Journal of Business Ethics 46, no. 4 (2003): 351–361.

[76]Bruce W. Tuckman, "Developmental Sequence in Small Groups," Psychological Bulletin 63, no. 6 (1965): 384.

[77]Ruth Federman Stein and Sandra N. Hurd. Using Student Teams in the Classroom: A Faculty Guide. Bolton, MA: Anker Publishing Company, 2000.

[78]Bill Eddy, Biff: Quick Responses to High Conflict People, Their Hostile E-mails, Personal Attacks, and Social Media Meltdowns. Unhooked Books, 2011.

[79]Michael E. McCullough, Kenneth I. Pargament, and Carl E. Thoresen, Forgiveness: Theory, Research, and Practice. Guilford Press, 2001.

[80]Richard N. Redinger, "Fat Storage and the Biology of Energy Expenditure." Translational Research 154, no. 2 (2009): 52–60.

[81]Stephan Guyenet, "Fast Food, Weight Gain, and Insulin Resistance." Whole Health Source: Fast Food, Weight Gain, and Insulin Resistance (blog), May 22, 2011 (2:33 p.m.), http://wholehealthsource.blogspot.com/2011/05/fast-food-weight-gain-and-insulin.html.

[82]Richard Johnson, Mark Segal, Yuri Sautin, Takahiko Nakagawa, Daniel Feig, Duk-Hee Kang, Micahel Gersch, Steven Benner, and Laura Sanchez-Lozada, "Potential Role of Sugar (fructose) in the Epidemic of Hypertension, Obesity and the Metabolic Syndrome, Diabetes, Kidney Disease, and Cardiovascular Disease." The American Journal of Clinical Nutrition 86, no. 4 (2007): 899-906.

[83]"Trends in Intake of Energy and Macronutrients—United States, 1971–2000." The Journal of the American Medical Association, 53, no. 4 (2004): 1193–194.

[84]Kris Gunnars, "How Many Calories Should You Eat Per Day to Lose Weight?" Authority Nutrition, accessed January 6, 2014, http://authoritynutrition.com/how-many-calories-per-day/.

[85]Kris Gunnars, "9 Ways That Processed Foods Are Slowly Killing People." Authority Nutrition, accessed January 6, 2014, http://authoritynutrition.com/9-ways-that-processed-foods-are-killing-people/.

[86]Kris Gunnars, "Added Sugar Is The Single Worst Ingredient in The Diet. Period." Authority Nutrition, accessed January 6, 2014, http://authoritynutrition.com/sugar-the-worst-ingredient-in-the-diet/.

[87]Nicole M. Avena, Pedro Rada, and Bartley G. Hoebel, "Evidence for Sugar Addiction: Behavioral and Neurochemical Effects of Intermittent, Excessive Sugar Intake." Neuroscience & Biobehavioral Reviews 32, no. 1 (2008): 20–39.

[88]Matthias Schulze, JoAnn Manson, David Ludwig, Graham Colditz, Meir Stampfer, Walter Willett, and Frank Hu. "Sugar-sweetened Beverages, Weight Gain, and Incidence of Type 2 Diabetes in Young and Middle-aged Women." Journal of American Medicine, 292, no. 8 (2004): 927–34.

[89]Vasanti Malik, Matthias Schulze and Frank Hu. "Intake of Sugar-sweetened Beverages and Weight Gain: A Systematic Review." 84 (2006): 274–88.

[90]Kris Gunnars, "10 Disturbing Reasons Why Sugar Is Bad For You." Authority Nutrition, accessed January 6, 2014, http://authoritynutrition.com/10-disturbing-reasons-why-sugar-is-bad/.

[91]Kris Gunnars, "Fruit Juice Is Just as Unhealthy as a Sugary Drink." Authority Nutrition, accessed January 6, 2014, http://authoritynutrition.com/fruit-juice-is-just-as-bad-as-soda/.

[92]Kris Gunnars, "Saturated Fat: Good or Bad?" Authority Nutrition, accessed January 6, 2014, http://authoritynutrition.com/saturated-fat-good-or-bad/.

[93]Kris Gunnars, "6 Graphs That Show Why The 'War' on Fat Was a Huge Mistake." Authority Nutrition, accessed January 6, 2014, http://authoritynutrition.com/6-graphs-the-war-on-fat-was-a-mistake/.

[94]Kris Gunnars, "Do Low-Fat Diets Actually Work? A Critical Look." Authority Nutrition, accessed January 6, 2014, http://authoritynutrition.com/do-low-fat-diets-work/.

[95]Diann M. Ackard, Jillian K. Croll and Ann Kearney-Cooke. "Dieting Frequency among College Females: Association with Disordered Eating, Body Image, and Related Psychological Problems." Journal of Psychosomatic Research 52, no. 3 (2002): 129-136.

[96]World Health Organization. Guidelines for Drinking-water Quality: First Addendum to Volume 1, Recommendations. Vol. 1. World Health Organization, 2006.

[97]Kris Gunnars, "How to Lose Weight Fast: A Proven 3-Step Plan That Works." Authority Nutrition, accessed January 6, 2014, http://authoritynutrition.com/spt/how-to-lose-weight-fast-a-proven-3-step-plan-that-works/.

[98]H. Mintzberg, B. Ahlstrand, and J. Lampel, Strategy Safari: A Guided Tour Through the Wilds of Strategic Management. New York: Free Press, 1998.

[99]Jeffrey M. Ellenbogen, "Cognitive Benefits of Sleep and their Loss Due to Sleep Deprivation." Neurology 64, no. 7 (2005): E25–E27.

[100]Francesco Cappuccio, Frances Taggart, Ngianga-Bakwin Kandala, Andrew Currie, Ed Peile, Saverio Stranges, and Michelle Miller, "Meta-Analysis of Short Sleep Duration and Obesity in Children and Adults." Sleep Duration and Weight 31, no. 5 (2008): 619–26.

[101]Steven Greenhouse, "Report Shows Americans have more Labor Days." New York Times, accessed January 6, 2014, http://www.nytimes.com/2001/09/01/national/01HOUR.html.

[102]David C. K. Roberts "Quick Weight Loss: Sorting Fad from Fact." Medical Journal of Australia 175, no. 11/12 (2001): 637–640.

[103]M. R. Naghii, "The Significance of Water in Sport and Weight Control." Nutrition and Health 14, no. 2 (2000): 127–132.

[104]US Department of Health and Human Services. The Health Consequences of Smoking. 1988.

[105]Christopher Ellison and Jeffery Levin, "The Religion-Health Connection: Evidence, Theory, and Future Directions," Health Education and Behavior 25, no. 6 (1998): 700–20.

[106]A.A. Services and Alcoholics Anonymous. Alcoholics Anonymous: The Story of How Many Thousands of Men and Women have recovered from Alcoholism. (Hazelden Publishing, 2001).

[107]Lynell Burmark and Lou Fournier, Enlighten Up!: An Educator's Guide to Stress-Free Living, (Association for Supervision and Curriculum Development, Alexandria, VA: 2003).

[108]Peter C. Canellosand Edward D. Kleinbard. "Miracle of Compound Interest: Interest Deferral and Discount after 1982" Tax L. Rev. 38 (1982): 565. See also, Marc Eisenson, A Banker's Secret: The Booklet that can save you Thousands of Dollars on your Home Mortgage. (A Banker's Secret, 1984).

[109]George S. Clason, The Richest Man in Babylon. Giuseppe Castrovilli, 1955.

[110]Charles T. Clotfelter and Philip J. Cook. "Notes: The "Gambler's Fallacy" in Lottery Play." Management Science 39, no. 12 (1993): 1521–1525.

[111]D. E. Comings, R. Gade-Andavolu, N. Gonzalez, S. Wu, D. Muhleman, C. Chen, P. Koh, et al. "The Additive Effect of Neurotransmitter Genes in Pathological Gambling." Clinical Genetics 60, no. 2 (2001): 107–116.

[112]Denis Côté, Anne Caron, Jonathan Aubert, Véronique Desrochers and Robert Ladouceur, "Near Wins Prolong Gambling on a Video Lottery Terminal," Journal of Gambling Studies 19, no. 4 (2003): 433–438.

[113]Carolyn E. Schwartz and Rabbi Meir Sendor, "Helping Others Helps Oneself: Response Shift Effects in Peer Support," Social Science & Medicine 48, no. 11 (1999): 1563–1575.

[114]H. C. Bennet-Clark and E. C. A. Lucey "The Jump of the Flea: A Study of the Energetics and a Model of the Mechanism," Journal of Experimental Biology 47, no. 1 (1967): 59–76. See also, Zig Ziglar, See You At The Top. (Louisiana: Pelican Publishing Company, 2006).

[115] John R. Wooden and Steve Jamison. Wooden on Leadership. New York: McGraw-Hill, 2005.

[116]John Wooden, My Personal Best: Life Lessons from an All-American Journey. (McGraw Hill Professional, 2004).

[117]Peter M. Gollwitzer, "The Volitional Benefits of Planning." The Psychology of Action: Linking Cognition and Motivation to Behavior, 13 (1996): 287–312. See also, David Allen, Getting Things Done: The Art of Stress-free Productivity, (Penguin, 2002).

[118] Jan Born, Kirsten Hansen, Lisa Marshall, Matthias Mölle, and Horst L. Fehm. "Timing the End of Nocturnal Sleep." Nature, 397, no. 6714 (1999): 29–30. See also, Henriette Anne Klauser, Write it Down, Make it Happen: Knowing what you want and getting it. (Simon and Schuster, 2001).

[119]George A. Steiner, Strategic Planning. (Simon and Schuster, 2010). See also, Keri K. Stephens, Jaehee K. Cho and Dawna I. Ballard. "Simultaneity, Sequentiality, and Speed: Organizational Messages about Multiple-Task Completion." Human Communication Research 38, no. 1 (2012): 23–47.

[120]Herbert L. Mirels, "Dimensions of Internal versus External Control." Journal of Consulting and Clinical Psychology 34, no. 2 (1970): 226. See also, Kirsten Lagatree, Checklists For Life: 104 Lists To Help You Get Organized, Save Time, and Unclutter Your Life. Kirsten Lagatree, Pu." (1999): 320.

[121]Colin F. Camerer and Robin M. Hogarth. "The Effects of Financial Incentives in Experiments: A Review and Capital-labor-production Framework." Journal of Risk and Uncertainty, 19, no. 1–3 (1999): 7–42. See also, Malcolm Gladwell, Outliers: The Story of Success. (Penguin UK, 2008).

[122] Edward T. Linethal and Tom Engelhardt, History Wars: The Enola Gay and Other Battles for the American Past. Macmillan, 1996.

[123]Godelieve Mercken-Spaas, "Destruction and Reconstruction in Hiroshima, mon amour." Literature/Film Quarterly 8, no. 4 (1980): 244.

[124]Godelieve Mercken-Spaas, "Destruction and Reconstruction in Hiroshima, mon amour." Literature/Film Quarterly 8, no. 4 (1980): 244.

[125]B. Franklin, Poor Richard's Almanack. New York, NY: Barnes & Noble Publishing, 2004. V. Frankl, Man's Search for Meaning. Boston, MA: Beacon Press, 1992.